INNER *GAME*

Breaking Golf's Unbreakable Barriers

by

Dr. Mac Powell

Dark Bird Press
Los Angeles

©2004 Dark Bird Press

PO Box 4762 Culver City, California 9023

To place an order visit our Web site at::
WWW.INNERGAME.ORG

Layout and illustrations by Daniel Rhone.
Edited by Heather Noggle.

Library of Congress Control Number: 2004093223

First Paperback Edition
ISBN 0-9755212-0-9

for

God and Bobby Jones

PROLOGUE

Personality rules performance in all athletic mediums, yet the paramount importance of personality in golf remains largely unnoticed and unaddressed. The significance of personality in golf is due to the individual "stand alone" nature of the game and its timing. In a four-hour round, a golfer is in the process of swinging the club less than five minutes. The rest of the time should be devoted to mastering the mental game, overcoming the limits of personality, and maximizing physical assets. Golfers regularly fail to see the limits of their personality and become patterned, repeating inconsistent performance after inconsistent performance.

Optimizing performance requires understanding your personality and its tendencies, and recognizing that there is no room for mental preparation once you've addressed the ball. You must have prepared for the shot well before you begin your pre-shot routine, before you've entered the course, before you've finished your practice at the range.

The problem is not that personality determines behavior, but that people are unaware of their personality's importance. All personalities have strengths and weaknesses, and all personalities have unique tendencies that make slipping into the zone easier if you are aware of the mechanisms.

Enhanced performance in any sport, but particularly golf,

requires understanding and mastering the way personality and mental processes determine particular outcomes. This book addresses personality in terms of Types, unique characteristics that form the what of who we are. Once you have a grasp of who you are and what particular tendencies you have in performance, the book offers a set of Basic Skills and Skills for Mastery that will assist golfers of varying abilities with mastering the mental game. Exercises in the back of the book offer practical technical solutions, drills and practice aids, personality inventories, and worksheets to assist players to maximize their mental and physical efforts on the course.

At its core, this book is a spiritual endeavor drawing from the wisdom of my teachers, many of whom were tremendous golfers, but all of them were tremendous people. My thanks to all of you who have assisted in the development of this book and to those of you who will grow by reading it.

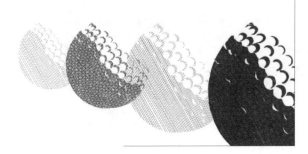

THE
TYPES

The following section describes the Types, illustrating each with historical examples, and how aspects of the self and personality affect performance. Subsequent sections address more practical skills and offer Type-specific exercises designed to maximize optimal performance.

One of the assumptions of this book is that our unique strengths, weaknesses, barriers, and roles are familiar. We've grown accustomed to repeating them. The patterns we create have meaning, particularly in our relationships and in our passions. Some of us repeatedly compliment other people, receive positive feedback from those compliments, and unendingly repeat that cycle. From this pattern we might assign the belief that we are considerate and thoughtful, and yet this is not all of who we are. The truth is that we are both considerate and inconsiderate, empathetic and selfish. Unbeknownst to you, your personality has established the limits of who you are and how far you'll go in life: whom you'll marry, how high and how fast you'll climb the corporate ladder, and whether you'll ultimately be satisfied or disappointed with your life. This highlights an underlying assumption of my work, that **you will go only as far in golf as you go in your life**.

The link between worldly success, golfing ability, and spiritual fulfillment is found in how we use, develop, and learn from our personalities. This link has a tremendous amount to teach you.

For this book, I have identified nine distinct personalities, or Types. The model is based upon the Enneagram, an ancient system for understanding personalities rooted in Jungian Psychology. The basics are quite simple. There are nine Types, all with strengths and weaknesses that manifest in consistent and habitual patterns of thoughts, feelings, and actions. Our Type makes us predictable, but often only to the people around us. We are the last to see how our personality hinders our progress.

The Types are unique expressions of who we are. Each of us has a dominant Type, a particular lens that we see the world though, and each of us has traits and tendencies that cause us to identify with other "Types" of people in very specific and predictable ways. Early in our lives, we adopted particular Types, almost always as a reaction to what was happening in our families. Over the course of our lives, we incorporate the positive traits of other Types, but remain, almost without exception, an expression of the dominant Type developed in our childhood.

My hope is that you will identify with each of the Types, but that you will choose one that exemplifies your own personality and idiosyncrasies as a golfer and person. It will be helpful for you to remind yourself, your friends, and your playing partners of your tendencies, to tell them who you are so that they can assist you with monitoring your growth. It is my hope that you can begin to see movement, and that you can begin to alter your perception of yourself and others. Each Type can thrive in any setting, and mastering how you react to situations and people in your life will assist you both on and off the course. The game has much to teach, and students are rewarded as much for attitude and approach as their actual performance.

Player Type:

The **CRUSADER**

Crusaders are responsible, serious, and self-disciplined. At their best, they are tolerant and accepting, fair and principled, yet their strong opinions are sometimes accompanied by impatience and sarcasm, and, not surprisingly, Crusaders are no strangers to conflict. Crusaders are often model children who grow into hard working, righteous, and fiercely independent adults. Crusaders use their minds more than their hearts, and often intellectualize emotional problems and regularly repeat unsuccessful attempts to solve feeling problems with thinking solutions.

Crusaders can feel agitated over the little things in life and spend an extraordinary amount of energy investing in what is scrupulous or correct. This can lead to disappointment or resentment toward others who seem to sail easily through life. The major character flaw of the Crusader is anger or rage, reacting to the injustices or inefficiencies around him with outward demonstrations of self-righteousness.

On the golf course, the Crusader is conscientious, fair, serious, and committed to improving his game. As a student of the game, the Crusader may be its most rigorous practitioner, constantly seeking innovative ways to improve upon technique and tirelessly devoted to established practice routines. Crusaders are excellent critics, but their devotion to perfectionism and reluctance to accept the difficult transformations in demeanor and mental approach can inhibit long-term performance. From a technical standpoint, Crusaders are likely to lose focus of rhythm, tempo, and fluidity, and attempt to solve problems on the course with rigidly held swing thoughts, regardless of the outcome.

In order to develop into great players, Crusaders often attempt to think their way out of bad habits or decisions; however, the key to improved performance is a recognition of a Crusader's passions and emotions and a commitment to the enjoyment of the processes of improvement rather than the destination of perfection.

"I do not play to break records. I play to win. I think the Lord has let me win for a purpose. I hope that purpose is to give courage to those that are sick or injured or broken in body."

- Ben Hogan

William Benjamin Hogan was the prototypical Crusader. Arguably the best ball striker and precision shot-maker in the game's history, Hogan stood five-seven and weighed a mere 135 pounds. His ability to focus during competition was known as the "Hogan trance," and the mystique that followed him was largely responsible for his professional success.

Hogan's early life is as exemplary as his professional career. His father committed suicide when Hogan was nine, forcing Hogan to sell newspapers on the streets to provide for his family. The newspaper business was a good deal more cut-throat than it is today, and Hogan found himself in fist-fights to protect his turf from other paperboys. When he realized he could make more money caddying at the local golf course, he would run the seven miles to the course or sleep in the sand traps to be there before the fifty to sixty other children waiting for a bag. Bullies were common, and Hogan challenged the biggest of them to a fistfight in order to gain stature and maintain his place in the pecking order. Although it was difficult to find the resources or time to play, Hogan practiced earnestly, and in 1931 he gave up a job as a bank clerk to become a professional golfer.

Hogan's perfectionism was legendary. He would arrive days before an event to chart his way around the course. Hogan went bankrupt twice, and when he was on the verge a third time just before the 1938 Oakland Open, he considered retiring before shooting a final-round 69 to finish second. The prize was $380. "I played harder that day than I ever played before or ever will again," he said. His focus led to a tour money title in 1940, but his professional career was interrupted for three years while he served in World War II.

Although he didn't earn his first professional major until 1946, Hogan remained a consistent performer on tour until a near fatal car accident in 1949 when the car he was driving collided head on with a Greyhound bus. In an attempt to save his wife, Valerie, Hogan threw himself onto her as the car struck the bus. The impact drove the engine into the driver's seat and the steering wheel into the back seat of the car. While Valerie walked away without major injury, Hogan suffered a broken collarbone, a smashed rib, a double fracture of the pelvis, and a broken ankle. Numerous complications developed in the hospital and the Associated Press prepared an obituary, awaiting the news of Hogan's death.

Within a year of the accident, Hogan entered the Los Angeles Open. Although he wasn't expected to finish the tournament, he led until the seventy-second hole, when Sam Snead made a final birdie to force a playoff, which Hogan lost the following Monday. As the sports writer Grantland Rice said at the time, "Courage never goes out of style. His legs were not strong enough to carry his heart."

Hogan played the rest of his career bandaged and in pain. In 1950, eighteen months after the accident Hogan entered and won the U.S. Open, largely due to a remarkable 1-iron shot on the final hole to force a playoff, which Hogan won the following day by four strokes. At the time Hogan is reported to have said that, "People have always been telling me what I can't do. I guess I have wanted to show them. That's been one of my driving forces all my life."

Hogan was named Golfer of the Year for his comeback in 1950 and went on to win twenty-six more tournaments, including nine majors between 1948 and 1953. In 1953, he entered six tournaments and won five, three of them majors. In that year, he broke the Masters scoring record by five strokes, tied Bobby Jones as the only player to win four U.S. Opens, and won the British Open by a course-record breaking eight strokes. Of the British Open win Hogan said, "I do not play to break records. I play to win. I think the Lord has let me win for a purpose. I hope that purpose is to give courage to those that are sick or injured or broken in body." Hogan's motto was "work, study, endure," and his success was never a matter of chance. "I always outworked everybody. Work never bothered me like it bothers some people." A meticulous inventor and thinker, he found that by adding an extra spike to a section of the shoe on his right foot, he could improve his footing on the downswing, a retooling he would later credit as aiding his ball striking. A Crusader to perfection, he once dreamed he scored seventeen aces during a round, but woke up mad as hell because he hadn't aced the eighteenth hole.

In 1953, Hogan formed the Ben Hogan Company, and although it had many investors, Hogan demanded complete control over design and production of the products. His perfectionism almost bankrupted the company when he refused to let the first golf clubs go to market because they failed to meet his standards. When he died, Hogan's estate was valued at an astounding $100,000,000, a tribute to his work ethic and commitment to the highest of standards.

During a PGA Tour career that spanned five decades, Hogan played in 292 tournaments, accumulating sixty-three victories and nine major championships, including four U.S. Opens, two PGA championships, two Masters, and the British Open. Perhaps more amazing is that in ten years of competing in the U.S. Open, Hogan recorded four victories, two seconds, a third, a fourth, and two sixths. A member of the PGA Golf Hall of Fame and four-time PGA Player of Year, he is one of only five players to win all four Grand Slam titles.

Hogan was an iconic figure in golf, the standard for rigor and perfectionism. Throughout his life he used his high-mindedness and devotion to principle to prevail over poverty, poor performance, and injury. Crusaders overcome great obstacles in their lifetimes, yet it is often the near tragedies that fuel future success. After each stumble, Hogan became more focused and passionate. Despite small stature, Hogan triumphed over all life's challenges with heart, conviction, and pride in the day-to-day efforts of his life.

Player Type:

The **ADVISOR**

Caring, empathetic, and generous, the Advisor is the most gracious and forgiving of the Types. At his best, he is encouraging, humble, and supportive, yet the Advisor's need to feel wanted and appreciated for who he is can be overpowering, and may lead to people-pleasing and insincere praise. The Advisor is often the power behind the throne but may find himself asking questions about his true identity later in life. The Advisor's life revolves around people and relationships, and perhaps because Advisors are the most giving and sensitive of the Types, they are most susceptible to approval seeking.

The Advisor is the least likely to engage in fierce competition, yet his own game can become as impressive as any of the Types. Optimal performance typically occurs when playing or practicing alone, as introspection and grace are more easily achieved when not concerned with the presence of others. The Advisor is the least likely of the Types to master the game under competitive circumstances, and Advisors who become great players must first reconcile their own discomfort with the selfish practices required to free the time and energy necessary to develop as a player. If the Advisor's focus upon others can be set aside, or, better yet, redirected toward self-nurturing and support, the Advisor may be the most likely to achieve mastery in a short period of time, as he is already capable of many of the critical elements of mastery: empathy, acceptance, and a deep passion for the game.

"Don't think you really win until you live up to that high thing within you that makes you do your best, no matter what."
-Patty Berg

Advisors are counted as the game's foremost teachers, and in addition to her impressive accomplishments on the course, no man or woman has grown the game or touched as many lives as Patty Berg. Born in Minnesota in 1918, Berg was a skilled athlete throughout her childhood, competing in numerous sports before turning to golf as a full-time passion at the age of thirteen. She was a perennial contender in state and U.S. Amateurs and won the U.S. Women's Amateur in 1938. After turning professional in

1940 when only a handful of women played on the fledgling tour, she was injured in a car accident that required two resettings of her left knee. After eighteen months of rehabilitation, she entered the Marines for two years, completed cadet school as a second lieutenant, and went on to win the first U.S. Women's open in 1946.

When the LPGA was formed in 1948, Berg joined the Didrickson Zaharias, Betty Jameson, and Louise Suggs as the Big Four of women's golf, dominating the tour throughout the next two decades. Berg would win seven times that first year while serving as the LPGA's President. In her career, she led the tour in money three times, won the Vare Trophy for lowest scoring average three times, and was three times voted outstanding woman athlete of the year by the Associated Press. She is the first woman to win $100,000 in career earnings and in 1963 received the highest honor of the USGA, the Bob Jones Award.

Berg was a small woman at 5'1," but had shotmaking precision that rivaled Byron Nelson. Carol Mann reportedly said that Berg was, "the most knowledgeable person, man or woman, of different golf shots that [she had] ever known." Berg played competitively until the age of 62, but more impressive than her fifty-seven professional titles are her contributions to the game. She instructed over 10,000 clinics in her lifetime, making her perhaps the most influential teacher the game has known. Berg's contributions on and off the course were a reflection of her generous heart and personable nature.

There were four great founders of women's golf and it

would have been easy for Berg to have been forgotten by historians, yet her solid game and stellar accomplishments were merely a reflection of the deeper value she held as a person. A true Advisor, her charisma and giving spirit are largely responsible for the success of women's golf world-wide, and her devotion to the ideals of the game were in large part responsible for her success as competitor and person.

In 1978, the LPGA established the Patty Berg Award, given to the female golfer who has made the greatest contribution to women's golf during the previous year. Her spirit of generosity, support, and kindness made Patty Berg the ideal Advisor.

Player Type:

The **ACHIEVER**

For Achievers, failure is not an option. Almost without exception, Achievers will quickly master the rudimentary elements of the game, giving them a leg up on the rest of the Types. Achievers are competent, goal-oriented, ambitious, organized, and performance driven. At their best Achievers are well-adjusted, both self-accepting and interested in the affairs of others. Achievers want the right job, best car, most impressive home, and will spend a great deal of time choosing and creating the foundation for an impeccable family. The Achiever is a go-getter and a model citizen, yet may ignore the emotional nuances of life and relationships.

The weakness of the Achiever is the natural byproduct of quickly found success. Because golf is a game that will ultimately require acceptance and humility, the Achiever may try to bypass these virtues in favor of perfectionism or an irrational dedication to technical mastery. For the Achiever, the limits his abilities are painful reminders of his humanity and the edges are either quickly conquered or expertly avoided. Achievers often have a love-hate relationship with the game and find themselves going through phases of intense devotion and avoidance of the game.

"What I have learned about myself is that I am an animal when it comes to achievement and wanting success. There is never enough success for me."

-Gary Player

Exemplars of the Achiever include three of the biggest names in golf: Tiger Woods, Gary Player, and Jack Nicklaus. By almost any measure, Nicklaus is the greatest among these, perhaps the greatest among any. Of his victory at the 1965 Master's Bobby Jones said that Nicklaus, "plays a game with which I am not familiar." Combining tremendous physical ability with boundless psychological resources, Nicklaus set the standard for optimal performance under the greatest of pressures. Playing against giants in the history of the game, Nicklaus emerged far ahead of the competition, yet his ultimate genius was that he won by never beating himself. Nicklaus' combination of explosive shotmaking and conservative management calculating the course, his opponent, and how he was playing at the moment made him the most feared competitor of the late 20th Century.

Between 1962 and 1986, Nicklaus won seventy official events on the PGA Tour, two U.S. Amateurs, and eighteen majors: a record six Masters, a record-tying four U.S. Opens, three British Opens, and a record-tying five PGAs. He completed the Career Grand Slam three times, something no other player has done more than once. If performance in major championships is the ultimate criterion of a career, then no golfer has made a mark like Nicklaus.

Nicklaus was born in Columbus, Ohio in 1940 and enjoyed an almost unmatched amateur career. Between his U.S. Amateur victories, he tied for second at the 1960 U.S. Open. By the time he turned pro, Nicklaus weighed an unseemly 215 pounds, yet his controlled driving and unmatched long-iron play set him far ahead of his competitors. By 1967, he had won seven majors. After shedding much of his unwanted weight in the late 1960's, he won seven more majors between 1970 and 1975. He led the Tour money list eight times, twice while playing only 16 events and between 1962 and 1979 he finished in the top ten in 243 of the 357 official events he played in.

In addition to his explosive power and precision shotmaking, Nicklaus' ability to gather himself during decisive moments separated him from his peers, nowhere more evident than in his back-nine 30 at the 1986 Masters, where, at the age of 46, Nicklaus put together a final-round 65 to win by one.

Hall of Famer Gene Sarazen, on speaking of Nicklaus,

offered, "I never thought anyone would ever put Hogan in the shadows, but he did. Nicklaus has the remarkable combination of power and finesse, and he is one of the smartest guys ever to walk the fairways. Jack Nicklaus is the greatest competitor of them all." As graciously as he won, he was equally magnanimous in defeat, finishing second in nineteen majors, and always giving credit to the winner.

Nicklaus' talent and mental preparation are iconic, yet like Palmer, he credited his success to his wife and family. For Achievers, finding a balance between the pressures of performance and the natural surrender to life's beauty and uncertainty is the only escape from the neuroses of perfectionism. Nicklaus found the balance by separating golf from home and family, and gave each their due so that they supported one another. Perhaps more than any of his golfing accomplishments, Nicklaus' ability to grow a healthy marriage, five children, and sixteen grandchildren mark him as the most accomplished of Achievers.

Player Type:

The **MYSTIC**

The Mystic is the most inwardly focused of the Types. Mystics are often quiet, elegant, imaginative, and capable of passionate self-expression. For this reason, they are often seen as feeling types and direct these feelings toward a variety of endeavors, some creative others self-destructive. Mystics believe that the authentic life is the only one worth living, and can find peace and meaning in even the most difficult of human conditions. Mystics pursue the impossible dream out of a deep need for understanding and feeling, and the well from which they draw is filled with passion for the unfulfilled promise of wholeness and what is missing in life.

The Mystic is the most streaky Type, without question. It is hard to say what drives the Type to greater heights, shame or self-pretension. Mystics can be dangerous competitors, and when encouraged and challenged by the right coach, I suspect that the Mystic has the potential to be the greatest golfer of the Types.

"My wife and my children came first; then my [legal] career; finally, and never in a life by itself, came golf."
                              -Bobby Jones

Robert Tyrne Jones was born in 1902, the son of a beloved Atlanta lawyer, whom everyone affectionately called "Colonel." A fine golfer in his own right, the Colonel was a low-handicapper who had once been drafted by a team that would later become the Brooklyn Dodgers. One of Jones' fondest memories was meeting his father in the club championship at the age of 13, outlasting his father in the event. Despite being perhaps the greatest player in the history of the game, Jones pursued many interests. His degree in engineering at the age of eighteen was followed three years later by a degree from Harvard College in English, which he earned in just three semesters. In 1924, Jones attended Emory University Law School. After only one year of study, he sat for and passed the state bar exam, leading to his subsequent withdrawal from law school to take a position in his father's firm. It was during this same year that Jones married his childhood sweetheart at the age of twenty-two. The couple's family grew significantly through the years, adding three children, the eldest of whom went on to compete against Jack Nicklaus in the U.S. Amateur Qualifier.

As a golfer, Jones had no weaknesses. His power was as great as any player in the game, yet his touch around and on the greens were unmatched. His languid swing came from a stance that was incredibly narrow, allowing for tremendous hip rotation in comparison to the modern golf swing. To gain more distance, Jones would simply elongate the backswing, yet never hurrying to or through the downswing. As a golfer, Jones was a giant. In the 1920s, he was "an ultra-athlete," according to historian Charles Price, "recognized at being better at this game than any other athlete was at his."

Beginning with his victory in the 1923 U.S. Open and ending with his U.S. Amateur victory at Merion in 1930, Jones won thirteen championships in twenty tries, the most imposing run of major titles the game has ever seen. His crowning glory was The Grand Slam of 1930, in which he became the only golfer ever to win U.S. Amateur, British Amateur, British Open and U.S. Open in the same year, in fact, the only golfer to win all four in a career. What is perhaps most remarkable about his accomplishments is that he never played competitive golf more than three months in a year at any point in his life. In hindsight, what is most telling about Jones' mental approach is his intensity. It was not unusual for Jones to lose as much as eighteen pounds during a tournament. After wining the 1926 U.S. Open, he inexplicably broke into tears in his hotel room, buckling under the strain of the week. His fiery temper as a youth was legendary, and his mastery of his inner game was the impetus for his mastery in his young adult life.

While his accomplishments on the course speak volumes, his everlasting testament to the game sits on 365 acres of land once known as Fruitlands Nursery. Of the land that became Augusta National, Jones said, "It seemed that this land had been lying here for years just waiting for somebody to lay a golf course upon it. Indeed, it even looked as though it already were a golf course." Collaborating with Dr. Alister Mackenzie, the two designed the greatest course on the continent. In historical terms, building Augusta National was designed for a somewhat selfish purpose; Jones was no longer able to play golf without attracting hundreds of spectators, and golf with his friends became impossible. Augusta was intended to be a private club where he could play in peace, yet in 1933, Jones opened the course, by invitation, to a select group of players. The membership had discussed the idea of hosting a U.S. Open, but the USGA always held the event in June or July, periods of unbearable heat in Atlanta and the town of Augusta was not yet equipped to host a major tournament. Instead, cars from thirty-eight states filled the lots to see Jones among the field of elite players. Although he finished tied for thirteenth, the event was a smashing success, and the event would become, five years later, The Masters.

Jones authored hundreds of syndicated newspaper columns, and with the help of journalist O.B. Keeler, published Down the Fairway, a book that went into a third printing within two months. More than any player in history, Bobby Jones is the model of the complete golfer.

Supremely gifted, Jones was a man of vast intelligence and profound character. Herbert Warren Wind wrote that, "In the opinion of many people, of all the great athletes, Jones came the closest to being what we call a great man."

In 1948, he developed syringomyelia, a fluid-filled cavity in his spinal cord causing first pain, then paralysis. Jones never played golf again and was eventually restricted to a wheelchair until his death in 1971.

Golf historians rightly marvel at Jones' accomplishments. How does a man master so many endeavors with such grace? I believe Jones' early temperament, fiery and wild, was later tamed by deep spiritual conviction. He surrendered to his mortality and the inevitability of his aging and left competitive golf while he could remember his mastery. Like other successful Mystics, he overcame life's challenges by balancing intense passion with devote surrender. If not the greatest golfer of all time, he remains the greatest of golf's Mystics, defying and creating, expanding and growing the game through his generosity, humility, and loving spirit.

Player Type:

The THINKER

Inquisitive, profound, perceptive, and unsentimental, the Thinker, like the Mystic, is prone to complexity and self-reliance, yet the Thinker is the more playful of the two types. Thinkers are skilled at reason and rationalization and regularly find themselves racked with anxiety and self-doubt both on and off the course. They are the most visionary of the Types, pioneers in approaches to the game.

Thinkers can be private and shy, and may turn silent around strangers. Even around friends, Thinkers often watch what they say and may regularly take the stance of neutral observer. When the Thinker does speak, he is precise and exact. Others will listen. Thinkers' feelings are rarely displayed, and though they have as many as any of the Types, they are often too delicate, precious, and private to be displayed for others. Thinkers are meticulous planners who thrive in situations with predictability. They are prone to specialization in obscure hobbies or careers that help to explain the complexities of existence and uncertainty.

The Thinker is often devoted to the ideas of the game rather than to the experience or performance of it. His inward and sometimes detached approach can lend him to preoccupation with impractical or extreme beliefs or desires. Yet, here is the strength of the Thinker. His fuel and commitment to ideas can be long-reaching, and if allowed to be steadily focused, there is no height he cannot reach.

"Every great player has learned the two Cs: how to concentrate and how to maintain composure."

-Byron Nelson

Among the many golfers who have carried this Type, Byron Nelson stands out as the greatest Thinker of the game. Nelson's streak of 11 victories in a row in 1945 is considered one of the untouchable records in professional athletics. He finished the 1945 season with eighteen victories, seven second-place finishes, and nineteen consecutive rounds under seventy, the greatest single season accomplishments in the history of the game.

Nelson was born in 1912 just outside Waxahachie, Texas. He and Ben Hogan both caddied at the same country club, where young Byron defeated Ben in a playoff for the caddy championship in 1927.

Tall and broad with enormous hands, Nelson developed the techniques considered the basis for the modern swing. As steel shafts replaced hickory, Nelson found that the big muscles of the hips and legs produced a more powerful and consistent swing than the more wristy traditional swing. His more upright swing, full shoulder turn, and limited wrist cock produced ball striking that was so precise that when the USGA developed a mechanical device for testing equipment, it named it "Iron Byron." Before Nicklaus, it was Nelson who set the standard for judging distances with approach shots, one of the many visionary changes Nelson made to the technique of the game. Nelson kept meticulous notes after rounds and knew exactly where his game was and how to focus his energy upon deficiencies. "As a competitor, Byron was able to be mean and tough and intimidating--and pleasant," said Ken Venturi, whom Nelson mentored. "You can always argue who was the greatest player, but Byron is the finest gentleman the game has ever known."

In a relatively brief career, Nelson won fifty-four tournaments, including two Masters, two PGA Championships, and a U.S. Open. In the 1940's, he finished in the money 113 straight times and in seventy-five starts from 1944 to the end of 1946 won thirty-four times and finished second 16. In those three years, he finished out of the top ten just once. "Byron Nelson accomplished things on the pro Tour that never have been and never will be approached again," offered Arnold Palmer, who grew up idolizing the legend.

As impressive as Nelson's contributions were, he retired to a Texas cattle ranch at the age of 34 in 1946. Many Thinkers approach the game with a detached cynicism, but Nelson maintained an intense passion that he carried to competition. As that passion waned, he left the game, knowing with conviction that he had accomplished all he could. His passion for the game was passed on to the many amateur and professional students he has mentored over the last sixty years, imprinting his quiet but powerful force in the game throughout his life.

Player Type:

The **SKEPTIC**

The Skeptic is the most complicated of the Types, and Skeptics have the most difficult time finding peace in the game. Skeptics are fascinated by the "worst case scenario," which creates havoc in a golf swing. They are characterized by their hard work, devotion, and cautious approach to any endeavor. Skeptics are courageous, faithful, funny, and grounded; yet, of all the Types, the quickest to worry and find reasons for suspiciousness and blame. Thinking is the dominant function of the Skeptic, which often leads to anxiety and doubt. The Skeptic has the potential to learn the most from the game of golf, particularly its fickleness and seeming unfairness. Skeptics find relationships difficult and are always vigilant and watchful, even of their mates. They thrive in environments with clearly drawn structure and hierarchy, but may escape later in their careers to self-employment in order to avoid the scrutiny of supervisors. Skeptics can often be afraid to act on their own behalf and may replace doing with endless planning. They are suspicious of the motives of others and will often identify with underdog causes.

Skeptics seek safety, but in order to find mastery of the game, they must accept golf's uncertainty and cruelty as tests for continued dedication to their dreams and core beliefs.

"I was about five inches from becoming an outstanding golfer - that's the distance between my left ear and my right one."
-Ben Crenshaw

Ben Daniel Crenshaw was born in 1952 in Austin, Texas and showed early promise in Austin, winning the first tournament at age eight and capturing three junior state titles, three city championships, and the junior national title in 1968. Ben grew in the same town as future Hall of Famer Tom Kite, and the rivalry honed Crenshaw's competitive nature. Despite a tough exterior, Crenshaw's swing and putting stroke were fluid and natural, a testament to the teaching of his mentor, Harvey Penick.

Crenshaw played multiple sports in high school but found time to play up to thirty-six holes a day, ten months a year.

During his senior year, he finished 32nd at the U.S. Open, and went on to win eighteen of the nineteen tournaments he entered before attending the University of Texas in 1970. He capped his freshman year with an NCAA team and individual championship. "All through college, I've never had anything on my mind except golf. I can't get interested in anything else." He remained a Longhorn for three more years, capturing three NCAA individual titles before winning medalist honors at the PGA Tour Qualifying School in 1973.

Crenshaw won the first professional event he entered and took a second place finish three weeks later. He took two second-place prizes and finished in the top ten three other times in 1974 and tied for third at the 1975 U.S. Open, yet he was quickly lapped by the rest of the tour. Crenshaw met with former PGA Tour Professional Bob Toski, who focused on improving Crenshaw's mental attitude. Of the changes Crenshaw said, "I was about five inches from becoming an outstanding golfer - that's the distance between my left ear and my right one." The improved mental toughness led to four worldwide wins the following season and a second place finish on the PGA Money List.

Although Crenshaw continued to post PGA Tour victories, he was plagued by near misses in major championships, among them a third and two second place finishes at the British Open.

By 1982 Crenshaw had fallen to 83rd on the Tour Money List. "People were telling me all kinds of things and trying to help, but by then it was going in one ear and out the other

. . . I was a basket case." He abandoned the technical approaches and focused on vision and instinct to guide his shotmaking, resulting in a second place finish in the 1983 Masters and a win at the Byron Nelson weeks later. He carried the moniker Best Player Never to Win A Major only one more year before a victory in the 1984 Masters, finishing just ahead of his long-time competitor Kite.

His game deteriorated shortly after his major championship, due in part to the divorce from wife in the fall of that same year. Within months, Crenshaw was diagnosed with a hyperactive thyroid, requiring a long layoff for treatment. He led briefly at U.S. Open in Shinnecock Hills in 1986 and continued to capture PGA Tour victories throughout the 1980s and 1990s. Shortly after a practice round on the Sunday preceding the 1995 Masters, Crenshaw received news that his mentor Harvey Penick had passed away. Crenshaw flew to serve as a pallbearer at Penick's funeral only to fly back the same day to open the Wednesday tournament with a two-under par 70. Crenshaw fired rounds of 67, 69 to take the final round lead and held off Davis Love for a one of the most emotional victories in the history of the game.

Never the most physically gifted of athletes, Crenshaw's meager 5'9 160 pound frame supported an unparalleled mind and passion for the game. Gentle and easygoing he is one of the world's foremost collectors and authorities on the game of golf. He owns over 800 golf books and wrote the introduction to the 1982 special edition of Walter Simpson's The Art of Golf. His knowledge of English and Scottish courses is reported to be second to none, even among British scholars.

Crenshaw received USGA's Bob Jones Award in 1991 and captained American Ryder Cup Team to one of the most dramatic comebacks in sports history in 1999. He ended the Saturday night press conference on a fateful note: "I'm a big believer in fate. I have a good feeling about tomorrow. That's all I'm gonna say." He then got up and walked out of the press room.

Skeptics are streaky players and Crenshaw's career demonstrates that no amount of talent or knowledge guarantees success. When he played with detached conviction, as in the 1995 Masters, when he was able to play with his heart rather than his powerful mind, there was no barrier he couldn't overcome. Skeptics must surrender to the uncertainty of the game while holding faith in the process of practice and performance. As their worry fades, so do their performance barriers. Crenshaw's bouts of self-doubt, determination, perseverance, and ultimate triumph as a master of the game make him the prototypical Skeptic.

Player Type:

The **JOKER**

Curious, eager, outgoing, adventurous, and talkative, Jokers are the gluttons of the game, and their appreciation of the finer things makes them wonderful and entertaining playing partners. Jokers are the most gregarious of the Types, and their games often come from the easygoing approach they take with every challenge in their lives.

Jokers are the men who never grow up, who take pride in their individuality, and are often identified by their quick, if not always appropriate, wit. Jokers want to experience everything and are skilled at fitting together ideas and people from differing backgrounds and orientations. To all of this, they are charmers and flatterers of the worst sort.

Jokers tend toward risk taking and consistent performance is never as important as major accomplishments, if few and far between. Jokers are the best playing partners for a round on the weekend but don't mix well in competition with grinders and more introspective types. As students of the game, they can be fickle and spoiled with teachers who love their exuberance. To grow, they need discipline, structure, and a solid game plan that gives them the opportunity to take risks at appropriate times.

"I never wanted to be a millionaire. I just wanted to live like one."
-Walter Hagen

Walter Hagen was golf's greatest showman, a flamboyant, princely romantic who captivated the public and his peers with sheer panache. He was "Sir Walter," and "The Haig." His legacy as the most colorful character the game has ever seen often overshadows his titanic accomplishments.

Hagen was the first full-time touring professional. He won so often and with such grace and style that professionals soon overtook amateurs' status as the game's greats. As Arnold Palmer, the other great democrat of his sport, once said at a dinner honoring Hagen: "If not for you, Walter, this dinner tonight would be downstairs in the pro shop, not in the ballroom."

Hagen won eleven major championships, second only to

Jack Nicklaus' total of 18. Between 1914 and 1929, he won the PGA Championship five times (four of them in a row), the British Open four times, and the U.S. Open twice. Generally considered the greatest match player of all time, he once won twenty-two straight 36-hole matches in the PGA and, between the first round in 1921 and the fourth round of 1928, 32 out of 33. A pronounced sway in his swing often got his drives into trouble, but an unmatched ability to scramble and putt made him the world's most dominant player. He lived by the principle that "three of those and one of them still count four." After he defeated Bobby Jones 12 and 1 in a 72-hole challenge match in 1926, even Jones couldn't contain his frustration. "When a man misses his drive, and then misses his second shot, and then wins the hole with a birdie, it gets my goat." Jones is also credited as saying that he loved to play with Hagan because "he can come nearer beating luck itself than anybody I know."

When he was once told that an opponent he was to play the following day had already retired to bed, Hagan replied, "Yeah, but he ain't sleeping." Of Hagan, Paul Runyan said that "Hagen consistently beat the best professionals of his time and he wasn't afraid of Bobby Jones," no small feat in his time.

Born in 1892, Hagan's modest beginnings in Rochester, New York fueled his desire for a better life. The son of a blacksmith, he once said, "I never wanted to be a millionaire. I just wanted to live like one." His creed was that, "You're only here for a short visit. Don't hurry. Don't worry. And be sure to smell the flowers along the way." When he died in 1969, sports writer Charles Price echoed the love of the public for golf's most enthusiastic and regal ambassador, "He was splendid. They should have carried him out on a shield."

Hagan's enigmatic personality polarized fans of the game, and a lesser Joker might have taken personally the criticisms that he received for his irreverence. However, Hagan lived and died by the creed of the Joker: one is too many and a thousand is never enough. He supported his passion with solid preparation and a stoic commitment to remaining the greatest of golfers throughout his professional career.

Player Type:

The **MAVERICK**

Strong, resourceful, and independent, the Maverick is a pragmatic and action-oriented individual. Mavericks can be counted upon to reveal the truth, no matter how difficult. Because of this, they often step on toes, but make no mistake, they are loyal, inspiring, and gentle friends. They may fit the bad-boy or bad-girl archetype but are just as likely to be the loudest voice for a just cause.

The Maverick is a bold golfer and plays his own game. Mavericks are not distracted easily and are accurate judges of their own ability and trajectory. The limitations of the Maverick are his bluntness, and sometimes domineering adherence to their truth, which some may see as cynicism or defiance. Mavericks are excellent competitors and will tend to win close matches because of their vigilance and action-oriented approach to the game. The opportunity and challenge for the Maverick is to overcome his own perceptual framework, to see things from a different perspective, and to gain new methods and skill for his development as a player.

In some ways, Mavericks are the best students, because once they are convinced of an idea, they will work passionately to implement it; however, they can be stubborn and willful students if matched with the wrong coach or professional.

"When he gets going, it's almost as if Seve is driving a Ferrari and the rest of us are in Chevrolets."
-Tom Kite

Among his credits, Severiano Ballesteros won three British Opens and two Masters. He was also three-time European Golfer of the Year and led Europe to five Ryder Cup titles. In a 2002 interview, Seve told a reporter that then No. 1 ranked player Tiger Woods was "nothing special" and that his game was "light years away" from Ballasteros' game. Always brash and opinionated, Ballesteros exemplifies the Maverick.

Seve was born in 1957 in a small village in the north of Spain. All of his brothers had caddied at the Royal Pedreña

Golf Club, and all had turned professional. Seve's natural ability developed quickly, and he practiced tirelessly with a 3-iron that his brother Manuel had given to him. Seve would practice on the beach during the day and sneak onto the course at night. He won his first event when he was seventeen and won the European Order of Merit in 1976, largely because of a second place finish at the British Open at Royal Birkdale.

Ballesteros won the Order of Merit again in 1978 after winning six consecutive tournaments and captured his first British Open in 1979. He won the Masters twice, and of his victory at the 1983 Masters, Tom Kite said that, "When he gets going, it's almost as if Seve is driving a Ferrari and the rest of us are in Chevrolets." Ballesteros was undoubtedly the best player in the world for the better part of the next decade, winning the British Open in1984 at St. Andrews and again in 1988 at Royal Lytham St. Anne's. It was Ballesteros play at Royal Lytham St. Anne's that distinguished him as a Maverick, purposely driving into a parking lot to reach a green for an easy birdie. Ballesteros five World Match Play Championships and his unmatched record and enthusiasm for the Ryder Cup stand out among the career hallmarks of one of golf's greatest players.

In 1999, on the occasion of Severiano's induction to the Hall of Fame, Lee Trevino pointed out that: "Every generation or so there emerges a golfer who is a little bit better than anybody else. I believe Ballesteros is one of them ... On a golf course he's got everything - I mean everything: touch, power, know-how, courage and charisma." Ballesteros' powers of concentration were so great that he would barricade himself against the outside world weeks before a major championship, saying that people seemed to be talking to him as if through glass and that he rarely wouldn't hear the gallery or notice his competitors.

As one of the most enigmatic figures in the history of golf, Ballesteros exemplified the Maverick type. Although his renegade orientation and unwavering self-confidence led to professional success, Ballesteros, like many Mavericks, had difficulty with personal and professional relationships. Ironically, he played exceptionally well throughout his career in team events, particularly the Ryder Cup. As Ballesteros demonstrates, when Mavericks are able to give to friends, family, or causes greater than themselves, their focus and performance can be unstoppable.

Player Type:

The **PEACEMAKER**

The Peacemaker is the steady, easygoing player always gracious with a smile and intensely passionate about the game and relationships. At their best, Peacemakers are dynamic, self-aware individuals who can be the glue to a relationship, group, or corporation. Peacemakers may be slow to act but find progress through steady movement toward a given destination. At their core, Peacemakers fear that if they become angry or upset, people will not love or respect them. This drives a need for comfort and avoidance of conflict.

As golfers, Peacemakers tend to be surprisingly streaky players, in part because of an often unresolved anger or tension that comes from constantly holding back their own dreams and opinions for the good of others. Although this anger rarely or never surfaces overtly, particularly at home or work, you might see sudden and unpredictable outbursts out of a Peacemaker on the golf course. In fact, behind Jokers, Peacemakers are the most likely to throw a club. The Peacemaker's temperament gives him or her a 50/50 chance of real development as a player, and Peacemakers can find themselves waffling between true commitment to improvement, and complacency in favor of other activities. Once committed, there is no finer a player, and golfers of all levels will revel for an opportunity to regularly play with a professional of this type.

"I tried to look the whole gallery in the eye."
                                        -Arnold Palmer

Arnold Palmer is the father/grandfather of modern golf, an ambassador and archetypal Peacemaker. More than any athlete in its history, Palmer invented the game for the masses, and was recognized by the Associated Press as Athlete of the Decade for the 1960s. Palmer won 92 professional tournaments, 61 of them PGA Tour sponsored.

Palmer's magnetic personality drew fans by the thousands, and galleries of Arnie's Army saw victories at the U.S. Open, two British Opens, and four times at the Masters. Although he never captured the PGA Championship, he finished second three times. Between 1960 and 1963 he won twenty-nine titles and collected a then awe-inspiring $400,000.

He won the money title four times, played on six Ryder Cups, earning an astounding 22-8-2 record.

Palmer's impressive results on the course are dwarfed by his multi-million dollar interests in aviation, technology, course management, and golfing sales and manufacturing. Since the mid-1960s, Palmer has designed or built over 200 courses around the world. All of this from a man from a small industrial town in Pennsylvania, where he began playing golf at the age of four years old. His father, Milfred "Deacon" Palmer, worked as a golf professional and course superintendent, and Arnold worked in almost every capacity on his father's course beginning when he was 11 years old. Arnold went on to attend Wake Forest University and played on its golf team before entering the Coast Guard. While working as a salesman after being discharged from the Coast Guard he returned to the game, winning the 1954 U.S. Amateur. From his modest upbringing, Palmer broke down all of the class barriers in golf. After Ben Hogan growled, "How did Palmer get into this tournament," at the 1958 Masters, Palmer became an unstoppable force in professional golf.

Palmer's rivalry with Jack Nicklaus during the 1960s and 1970s can almost single-handedly explain golf's success today. In his rookie season, when Nicklaus tied Palmer at the 1962 U.S. Open at Oakmont, Palmer asked Jack if he wanted to split the purse prior to the 18 hole playoff the following day. Nicklaus said, "No Arn, let's just go play." Nicklaus would win the playoff and ultimately overtake the older Palmer, but the camaraderie and competitiveness of the two, their epic battles, set the stage for modern golf.

In any discussion of Palmer's life, the one name that cannot be overlooked is Winifred Walzer, who Palmer wed in the fall of 1954. Winnie traveled with him and their two daughters throughout his career and was the solidifying force in Palmer's hectic life. Upon her death in 1999 after a 13-month battle with cancer, President of the Golf Course Superintendents of America wrote that golf had lost the "first lady of the game."

Ambassadors and caretakers, the Palmers grew the game as the public's focus turned from amateur to professional events. Arnold's peaceful diplomacy, even more than his powerful drives, are in large part responsible for the state of the game today.

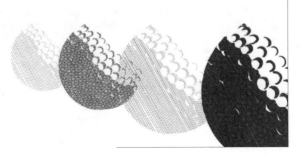

BASIC
SKILLS

Having identified a Type and knowing its strengths and weaknesses, the Basic Skills that follow serve as a foundation for the mental game. A series of Type-Specific exercises is also given toward the end of the book. My suggestion is to work on no more than one or two Basic Skills per week, and that you approach the Mastery Skills no sooner than six months after you've begun putting the Basic Skills into practice. All of the Basic Skills are required in order to achieve optimal performance. So, be thorough, patient, but hungry to grow.

IT'S OUT THERE

"A journey of a thousand miles must begin with a single step."

-Lao-Tsu

The road to improved performance in any endeavor begins with a dream. To achieve, you must believe. The road to your destination can be winding or direct. As a teacher, I hope that every student will learn with grace and ease. However, stubbornness, pride, incredulousness, jealousy, and sloth often make my students' journeys longer than they need be. To combat battling and resistance, I ask that every student Begin with a learning orientation to life. If you want to be a medical doctor, the most expeditious path would be to find a medical doctor and ASK how he or she obtained the lifestyle or profession you seek. If you wanted to be a painter, you would find and learn from a painter whose lifework you enjoy. It would be foolish for a person seeking to be a painter to ask a medical doctor for career advice. Although there are no doubt similarities in the way that a person from either profession overcame obstacles and achieved successes, it is most expeditious (or easiest) to learn from someone who has walked the path most similar to the one you are about to embark upon.

Seek out biographical material from a golfer or historical figure you admire. What made him stand out? What was his attitude? What resources did he draw upon? How did his deal with adversity and success? What were his goals and how did he pursue them? What were his guiding principles? What are the similarities and differences between yourself and your heroes? Whom did they trust?

If you don't already have a library card, go to the library and obtain one. Find a neighborhood bookstore and spend some time familiarizing yourself with the books you'd like to read or purchase, and spend time in the bookstore deciding which is which. Purchase only the books that will assist you in achieving your current life goal. Borrow the others from your local library. In other words, allow the money you spend to reflect your goals. If you check out How to Win Friends and Influence People from the library and purchase the latest hardbound copy of the latest John Grisham novel, you are sending the message that the latter is more valuable than the former. Make sure your words, actions, and SPENDING reflect the message you would like to send to yourself and others.

Optimal equipment is also important. If you don't have the tools necessary to maximize your unique potential, you are signaling that you're willing to fail. Maybe the reason is that holding onto money, or spending it on other things, is more important, or maybe that you cannot admit that your ball striking requires oversized irons or your putting requires a long putter. Either way, you've limited your development as a player by not realistically assessing what you need and spending the money, demonstrating that you are committed to a course of action.

Acquire consultation from an appropriate professional. A friend may know a lot about what you like to do or your relationship history, but he isn't likely to be a swing guru or sports psychologist. If you want to improve, find the best instruction you can afford. I was recently reading a quote by Lee Janzen speaking about how he paid "full price" for a Dave Pelz Short Game Seminar, and felt that it was worth every penny. In fact, what Janzen learned from Pelz he credited with his second U.S. Open victory. Even the greatest players in the world seek out instruction, and they're willing to pay for it, because it is valuable.

DRILL:

What does your spending say about your commitments?

1. Make a list of your daily expenses for one week. It doesn't have to be precise, but notice where you spend your money. At the end of the month, notice where you've spent the most. Is your money going to debt, to your children's schooling, to eating out, to movies or entertainment, to alcohol and drugs, or community charities? Where you spend your money says a lot about your commitments. How much do you spend on golf?

2. Commit at least 10% of your income to golf if you want to get better. When I began playing the game seriously I had very little money, but I devoted $200 every month to the game. This would go toward range balls, greens fees, and equipment. I tracked it on a credit card, and if at the end of the month I hadn't spent my $200, I went out and blew it on a nice round, new balls, or upgrading my equipment. As I began playing and achieving more on the course, I adjust-

ed the figure to $250. You don't have to spend a lot of money, but you need enough to be flexible, and to signal to the rest of the world: "Hey, this is important. I'm not going to compromise on this because this is valuable to me." Trust me, if you're worried about what your kids or your spouse are going to think, reframe it this way: What are you teaching your children by withholding from yourself? Do you want them to grow up running from their dreams and secret desires? Spending a little now, making a commitment to something you enjoy, teaches your children and the people around you that your beliefs and dreams are important. If they can't get that message, they're the ones out of balance.

> "Success, like happiness, cannot be pursued, it must ensue. And it only does so as the unintended side effect of one's personal dedication to a cause greater than oneself."
>
> - Victor Frankl

VISION

"A man's true delight is to do the things he was made for."

-Marcus Aurelius

Despite nearly 200 years of active practice and research, psychologists know very little about why people are so resistant to change. My experience has shown that change requires a focus upon the inner, as well as the physical and spiritual worlds. The history of great thinkers, inventors, and industrialists is the history of men and women who had a vision, and who surrounded themselves with people who supported them with emotional, spiritual, and monetary allegiance. The greatest of achievers achieved with the assistance of those around them and a deep conviction and spiritual belief. These are the same characteristics that will lead to achievement in your life, or on the golf course.

Complete the Vision Worksheet on the next page using the directions to follow:

VISION WORKSHEET

My character Type is: _____

My Greatest Inner Strengths: My Values:

1. _____   1. _____

2. _____   2. _____

3. _____   3. _____

4. _____   4. _____

5. _____   5. _____

My Assets: My Allies:

1. _____   1. _____

2. _____   2. _____

3. _____   3. _____

4. _____   4. _____

5. _____   5. _____

If God would grant a miracle and I could accomplish anything, it would be to:

_____

_____

_____

At my best, I am:

_____

_____

In order to stay my best, I need to:

_____

_____

Write a vision statement that reflects your dreams and values. Write it in the present tense, remembering that the more senses you incorporate, the more passionately the words leap off the page, and the more likely they will leap into reality.

My Inner Strengths: List your strengths. Any good explorer or captain of a seagoing vessel would know all of his assets before he sets out. Know yours.

My Values: Values can be anchors that hold you to the Earth when the sky falls. If your allies abandon you, if the world fails to support your idea, Values can be the life support for your dreams. But, your dreams and values must be aligned. If your deepest values are a hunger for money and you set out to be a missionary, the universe will not support you. In fact, you will likely be both a poor missionary and a poor person.

My Assets: In addition to your inner strengths, you possess tremendous assets. These might be your health, intelligence, sense of humor, physical strength, or monetary resources. Know your assets and continually revisit them with a sense of gratitude.

My Allies: This is likely the reason most people fail or succeed. If your friends and family do not support a course of action, you will see it undone. Surround yourself with those who accept you and your dreams, or better who will stand behind you as you achieve them. Beware of people who verbally support you, but who seem incredulous, or whose actions are not congruent with their verbal support. These people steal the energy from your dreams. Hold close your dreams and reveal them only to those people you know will not doubt or question them. Though this seems extreme, it is why great people succeed and others do not.

Know what you truly want and don't be afraid to ask for it. God doesn't differentiate big prayers from small prayers. He doesn't dole out his love in parcels, so don't be afraid to ask for what you truly want. Do you think God put you on Earth, in his image, to beg for table scraps? God put your dreams in you and is waiting for your call. Don't be afraid to ask for what you want. A mantra I used for several years was: My Dreams Come from God, and God has the Power to Accomplish Them.

Your Vision: There is nothing more powerful than a vision. The visions Christ received on Mount Sinai were vividly told to the apostles, and perfectly enacted by those surrounding him in his last days. Your visions should be as vivid, powerful, and personal. Dream small, achieve small. This doesn't mean that you should inflate your dreams and desires beyond what your soul feels is authentic. Your soul has a vision. If you tap into it, if you allow your creative visions, intuition, and energy to be struck like oil in a well the energy will rupture and dive to the surface. If you slow and restrict how the energy surfaces, if at all, it will become stagnate. Water in a river never stalls, is never stale. It gives life. Water that is dammed, is stuck and motionless, becomes putrid and useless.

Use motion, sensations, sights, smells, and sounds in your vision. The more clear and powerful the statement, the more clear and powerful the results.

> "Don't help me or serve me, but let me see it once, because I need it. Don't work for my happiness, my brothers—show me yours—show me that it is possible— show me your achievement—and the knowledge will give me the courage for mine."
>
> -Ayn Rand, The Fountainhead

PERSISTENCE VERSUS PERFECTION

> "If you make every game a life's or death proposition
> you're going to have problems. For one thing, you'll be
> dead a lot!"
>
> -Dean Smith

Bob Rotella makes an outstanding observation in one of his
book titles: Golf is Not a Game of Perfect. Any Touring
Professional will tell you that on a good day he will hit only
1 or 2 "perfect shots." The rest are misses, mistakes, errors,
faults, blunders, gaffes, slip-ups, and gaaks. And yet
Touring Pros rarely get flustered by their "slips." This is
because they have accepted that not every shot will be perfect, that even their best shots will not be received by the
greens and fairways in precisely the way they envisioned. I
believe the fastest way to improve an amateur's game is to
assist him with relinquishing the belief that every shot must
be perfect, that 250 in the fairway just isn't good enough
because someone else in his foursome hit it 300 (likely in
the rough). Golf is about staying focused in the present,
executing shots, accepting the results, and repeating the
process.

"Getting on a hot streak" is just as easy as "Getting on the
bogey train" if you take what your game and the course
offers. Several years ago I read an article in which Tom
Watson described his first time breaking 80. Instead of trying to hit perfect shot after perfect shot, he accepted a weak
slice and played to the middle of guarded greens. Not much
fancy about that, but persistence and a solid game plan
always beats trying to hit perfect pin-seeking shots that will

likely end up in trouble.

Another more global concept I would like to introduce is Trajectory rather than Goal. A goal is a very specific outcome. Wanting to shoot 65 is a goal. A trajectory is a statement about where you'd like to be heading. For example: "I'd like to continue to get better over time and feel proud about my progress." This is a trajectory statement. Even: "I'd like to play on a professional tour sometime in the future" is a trajectory. You can measure whether you're getting closer or farther from your trajectory by how you score, what kind of shots you can hit, and how calmly you perform under pressure. A trajectory leaves the possibility that your particular vision might not come to pass, that something better might be in store. A trajectory leaves room for grace, miracles, and change of direction.

One bad day on the golf course doesn't spoil a career. Even Greg Norman's melt down at Augusta in 1990 didn't stop him from continually playing at the highest level despite being well past 40 years of age. I think goals undid two of the most illustrious careers in pro tennis. Ivan Lendl wanted to win Wimbledon and Pete Sampras wanted to win the French Open BADLY. In fact, they structured their whole seasons toward the end of their careers just to win the events. Not to play well, not to build their game, but to win. When it didn't happen, year after year, I think both got discouraged, and it affected the way they approached and ultimately finished their career. Norman, on the other hand, desperately wanted to win Augusta, but his trajectory was to continue to be competitive week in and week out, and losing the Masters to his best friend Nick Faldo didn't deter him from continually trying to improve.

In 1945, Byron Nelson won 11 consecutive tournaments. During the streak, he never played a single practice round, and avoided the driving range between tournaments for fear of becoming "over-practiced." He could have pushed to become better or perfect, however he had perspective on his own process and accepted that he didn't need to be perfect, just persistent.

Relax, detach, and begin to plant the seeds for what you will grow. Decide on a trajectory and start asking yourself whether particular shots, particular reactions, and particular decisions bring you closer or farther from your trajectory. If you ask this question regularly, you will begin to see that perfection isn't required to be a great player. Simply understanding where you are and where you are going is the key.

DRILL:

1. Begin by being the envy of your foursome in mental attitude and fortitude. Your facial expression and eyes allow your playing partners to look inside. What do you want them to see: your doubt and fear or your quiet confidence and acceptance?

2. Spend a round just being aware of what you're conveying with your eyes and body language. See if anyone notices

any changes.

> "Golf is a game of mistakes. I made too many and let some of them bother me. You can't do that."
>   -Ben Hogan on faltering at the 1952 U.S. Open

SPEND YOUR UNITS

"I did never know so full a voice issue from so empty a heart; but the saying is true, 'The empty vessel makes the greatest sound.'"
                                                -William Shakespeare

"A full mind is an empty bat."
   -Branch Rickey, Major League Baseball Hall of Famer

In watching professional and amateur golfers, the greatest observable difference occurs in the moments just after a shot. Amateur golfers' heads snap up quickly, trying to find the ball, assess whether it's on line and just far enough, and whether it's going to go where they'd like it to. Professional players quickly deadlock the ball with their eyes and calmly watch it to its target, or in the case of one of the game's more forgotten great players, never see the ball at all. Bobby Locke, among the most accomplished of the game's players, is regarded as its greatest putter. Locke had an unusual style in that he NEVER WATCHED THE BALL GO TOWARD THE HOLE. When asked whether he wanted know which way the ball broke if he missed a putt, Locke simply asked "Why would I want to see the ball not go in the hole?"

Locke's technique is difficult for most players to accept. In fact, I've never had a student who could consistently keep his head down until the ball drops into the cup.

On a larger scale, if you're not exhausted after a round, you haven't given all of your energy on the course. I've never seen an athlete who's just accomplished something powerful not crash shortly thereafter, falling into a coach's arms or, in Tiger Woods' case, going straight to bed. If you've got reserve energy in your tank after a round, I want to know what you hoped to use it for, because that is what is important to you, not golf.

I played with a Hollywood agent many Sundays, and I kid you not, at the end of the round he was in his car returning calls and headed to evening cocktail meetings before my clubs were cleaned. He never improved as a golfer, but as an agent, he was spectacular. He made the choice to save his units for business, and most people make this choice. As a coach, however, I want these units. Those units make champions. When I work with couples trying to heal a relationship, I want their focus and energy on each other, on their communication, on the skills they're developing with each other. When I work with drug addicts, I want their energy in going to meetings, making sober friends, and finding a purpose greater than alcohol, crack cocaine, or crystal meth. It doesn't matter what activity draws focus, unless you spend your units carefully, specifically, and strategically, your game will not change. Your life will not change. Evaluating how much energy you have and spending it in a way that fits with your Vision and values is a critical component to optimal performance.

DRILL:

1. Spend an entire round not looking up after your putts. Notice the results, but more importantly notice how you feel as you wait for the sound of the ball falling into the cup. Is it confidence, fear, anxiety, or uncertainty? If you've spent your units, if you've studied the lie, contour, and speed of the putt, if you've executed the stroke as you've practiced it, you should be confident of the result. If you're not, review this skill again and begin to SPEND ALL OF YOUR UNITS.

2. Begin to notice how much energy you have in the morning and make a conscious effort to spend it strategically. If you only have 10 units, decide to spend them on positive goals rather than on trivial anxieties or unfulfilling hobbies or acquaintances. Be aware of your energy and hone how you spend it. If you wish to become a great player, you must devote at least 10% of your energy to the process each day, no matter what. If you have only a small amount each day, spend 10% visualizing particular performance outcomes. Where you spend your energy dictates the kind of outcomes you will see down the line.

"We must accept finite disappointment,
but we must never lose infinite hope"

Martin Luther King, Jr.

BE DECISIVE, BUT NEVER IN A HURRY

"Don't be in such a hurry. The little white ball isn't
going to run away from you."
-Patty Berg

Your first instinct is almost always correct. Doubt enters
when you try to outthink your gut reactions.
Microbiologists and physiologists have discovered that the
cells in your stomach and heart have the identical composi-
tion to the cells in your brain. In other words, your brain
isn't the only organ in your body with the ability to make
decisions. When you have a gut reaction, your body is
telling you something, and often, the message is more accurate and more in line with your best interests than the
thoughts from your brain. Deepak Chopra has said that this
is because the stomach has not evolved to the level of self-
doubt. Being decisive means having an awareness of your
bodily sensations and reacting without excessive mental
activity.

Great leaders are said to be decisive when they enact a well-
thought plan and stick to it, regardless of the consequences.
Being decisive on a golf course is no different. Ben Hogan
would never change his game plan regardless of the results.
He reacted to stimuli from his gut, not from mindful fear,
terror, or anxiety. And, he was never in a hurry.

Approach the ball like you know what you're about to do,
like you know where it's going. I once played and won a
match without hitting what I would consider to be a great

shot. My opponent told me as the match became dormie, "You really had it going today. You just looked so solid in your preshot routine, like you knew where every shot was going to go." In reality, I probably had as poor control over my shots as I had ever had, but my body language and my preshot routine never wavered. On that day, being decisive and not in a hurry won the match. When he dominated the world in the early 1990s Nick Faldo's opponents would regularly marvel at the way he approached and executed shots. They expected him to hit every fairway and every green. Never flustered, and never in a hurry, he executed shots to near perfection. However, when he was finished, he would admit that he only hit two or three perfect shots, and didn't make as many putts as he wanted. His attitude was confident, decisive, and never hurried.

DRILL:

This is one of the most exciting elements of the game that most players never consider. In baseball, a pitching coach will time the pitcher's delivery from the moment the throwing action is started to the moment the ball arrives in a catcher's glove. In golf, you should do the same. You should know exactly how long it takes from the moment you have evaluated the lie and decided upon a club to the moment the ball will land at the target. As in baseball, the time should be measured and known to within a fraction of a second. Think a moment what this would look like. There wouldn't be time for indecision, or reclubing, or rethinking the shot. It would be a programmed formula developed and rehearsed prior to stepping onto the course.

1. Devote at least five practice sessions of at least 25 minutes to this drill.

2. In your mind, begin counting seconds as soon as you have decided on a club. There are only a few critical elements that should take place because you would have already evaluated the lie.

> Decide on a target. Focus on the smallest possible point.

> Holding your eyes to the target, address the ball with your feet together. Make sure the ball is in the proper position in your stance.

> Find the target with your eyes.

> Align your club.

> Separate your feet the proper width.

> Find the target with your eyes.

> Check for tension in your body and release it as necessary.

> Take a slow breath.

> Find the target in your mind's eye.

Begin the swing.

Finish the swing to the target.

Hold your finish on the target.

See the ball landing and finishing on the target.

3. How long did that take? Use a stop watch or have some-one else time you, but don't use video for this exercise. Get in the habit of experiencing the process.

4. Break down the time for each element of your preshot routine.

5. Begin to practice this process, repeating it and timing the sequences perfectly.

6. When you have mastered this sequence, shotmaking and ballstriking will improve.

7. If in a round your timing gets unsettled, think about baseball. A batter will call timeout to upset a pitcher's rhythm and timing. If the wind, your playing partner, or your own mind upsets the natural rhythm you've estab-lished, your results will suffer. A major league pitcher will reset and begin his routine from the beginning if his timing is upset. Do the same. Never allow yourself to get out of the rhythm you've established in practice. The results would be failure.

TAKE TIME BETWEEN POINTS

"It does not matter how slowly you go, as long as you do not stop."

-Confucius

Jim Loehr, sports psychologist to many of tennis' best players during the 1990s, studied the habits of top-tied professionals and lower-tiered professionals and found no difference in their competitive habits during points. The difference was what occurred between points. Studying the IKG telemetry of the athletes, he found that in the 16 to 20 seconds between points, the heart rates of the top-tiered competitors dropped as much as 20 beats per minute. These players renewed their energy through rituals: walking back to the baseline in the same way, holding their heads high while relaxing their shoulders, focusing upon positive visual stimuli, and reinforcing their decisions with positive self-talk.

Research among top-tiered athletes has shown that cycling slowly through emotions, getting angry and staying angry, or being detached emotionally are not as effective as cycling gradually through the feelings of exhilaration and disappointment that occur during the course of a competitive event. Regrouping between shots, but not stuffing your feelings is a powerful tool on the course.

Jack Nicklaus speaks of his mental approach this way:

I was blessed with the ability to focus intensely on whatever I'm doing through most distraction and usually to the exclusion of whatever else might otherwise preoccupy me. Nevertheless, I can't concentrate on nothing but golf shots for the time it takes to play 18 holes. Even if I could, I suspect the drain of mental energy would make me pretty fuzzy-headed before the last putt went down. In consequence, I've developed a regimen that allows me to move from peaks of concentration into valleys of relaxation and back again as necessary.

My focus begins to sharpen as I walk onto the tee, then steadily intensifies as I complete the process of analysis and evaluation that produces a clear-cut strategy for every shot I play. It then peaks as I set up to the ball and execute the swing when, ideally, my mind picture of what I'm trying to do is both totally exclusionary and totally positive.

Unless the tee shot finds serious trouble, when I might immediately start processing possible recoveries, I descend into a valley as I leave the tee, either through casual conversation with a fellow competitor or by letting my mind dwell on whatever happens into it. I try to adhere to this pattern whether I'm playing my best or worst, but obviously have to work harder at it when things aren't going well.

DRILL:

There are many ways to distract and calm the mind, but the most effective is by becoming aware of your breathing. Try the following exercise between every shot for the last 9 holes of your next round. Compare your results to the previous 9 holes.

1. Take a slow full breath, allowing your chest cavity to expand. On the exhale, close your eyes and think of the most enjoyable vacation you ever took. Allow the breath to slowly leave your lungs.

2. With your eyes still closed, inhale again deeply. On the exhale, think of your favorite restaurant or meal, remembering a time when it was just right. Exhale slowly and evenly.

3. Eyes still closed, inhale and on the exhale, think of the person you love most in the world, and where you would like to be if you could be anywhere with that person. Exhale slowly.

Physiologists have found that no matter what your level of anxiety, performing this exercise will reset your internal rhythms, allowing your mind to focus on optimal performance.

NO "YEA BUT-ING"

"You must be the change you wish to see in the world."
-Mohandas Karamchand Gandhi

One of the first principles in this work is the power and importance of our words. "I can't" is almost always more accurately, "I won't." Barring physical and financial limitations, there are almost no "I can'ts." Therefore, acknowledge when you can't versus when you won't.

Words are powerful allies, but equally dangerous enemies. Too often in life we accept artificially imposed limitations, many of them reinforced by the words we use. We'd love to accomplish a particular goal, but immediately focus on our limitations. "Yeah, I'd love to go to play more often, but I don't have the time, money, or energy." I believe this is the most dangerous and self-defeating trick we use against our dreams. Similarly, we often undermine the gifts that others offer us in support of our dreams. If someone takes the time to offer you advice, or if someone has given you the time and attention to listen to your dreams and give you counsel, take it. This doesn't mean that you have to do what has been suggested. Give thanks to the other person's interest. A phrase that has helped me tremendously is "You might be right." This acknowledges the other person's concern and gives value to his intention to help. Besides, you may need that help in the future. Never say "Yeah, I could do that, but..."

"Everybody thinks of changing humanity and nobody thinks of changing himself."

-Leo Tolstoy

POSITIVE RITUALS

"The natural swing is something you create by hitting a million golf balls."

-Lee Trevino

Professional tennis player Ivan Lendl dominated his sport for a decade by devoting a tremendous amount of time to practice and positive rituals. Like Lee Trevino's notion of the natural swing, having a strong mental game is something developed over years of diligent practice. And remember what Ben Hogan said: "Every day you don't practice means it will take one day longer to meet your goals." Don't wait to develop good mental habits.

Lendl developed rituals for his fitness, including sprints, middle-distance running, bicycling, strength training, even ballet exercises to increase grace and balance. Additionally he adhered to a low-fat, high complex-carbohydrate diet and ate at very specific times.

Finally, Lendl practiced daily mental-focus exercises to improve concentration. He told his family and friends to not burden him with issues that might distract him and constantly focused on mental activities that kept him either fully engaged or strategically disengaged. Lendl meticulously scheduled time for relaxation and recovery, like a round of golf, afternoon naps, or massages. Lendl was so dedicated to his mental game that on the court he would he would visualize between points, developing a strategy that he would implement with exacting precision.

Developing Positive Rituals is an extension of the pre-shot routine, establishing the mind-body connection in such a way as to repeat positive, rather than random, outcomes. One of my first coaches told me that Practice Doesn't Make Perfect; Perfect Practice Makes Perfect. This exercise is designed to assist you in building positive rituals that you will use throughout your week, carry onto the golf course, use during your round, and assist you in regrouping after.

DRILL:

1. Review your Vision Worksheet and spend at least an hour completing the Barrier Worksheet located in the back of the book.

2. Spend some time reviewing the qualities of your strengths and values and consider when you have felt most empowered, either on or off the course. What were your thoughts? If you can, begin to replay your thoughts and feelings from back to front, traveling back in time. If possible, notice the moments that sparked your confidence of self-assurance. These are the thoughts that we want to encapsulate and recreate. These are the SPONSORING THOUGHTS, or the seeds from which positive outcomes will grow.

3. Make a list of Sponsoring Thoughts you would like to carry onto the golf course. Ideally, these would look something like "I will bring my best mental game with me today" or "I will carry 100% effort with me throughout the round,

and judge myself only on the degree to which I stayed focused on the noment and the shot before me." Or, these might be more ego-centered, something like, "I am successful, worthy, and vibrant and will manifest my best game yet." Write some sample Sponsoring Thoughts in your notes and review your Golf Vision Statement. Your Sponsoring Thoughts should ultimately be the triggering mechanisms for manifesting your Golf Vision.

4. Commit yourself to a 30-Day Action Plan to work on your barriers. Resolve that you will deal with your barriers off the course. By doing so, you are creating mental dividers that will compartmentalize the issues you must work on. Remember, though, you must deal with your barriers. Much like an inner-tube held under water, the harder you resist the changes you must make, the harder they will push back.

5. Begin to use your Sponsoring Thoughts regularly. Through repetition...results.

"We attract what we fear!"
                    -Anonymous

SLUMPBUSTING

"Slumps are like a soft bed. They're easy to get into and hard to get out of."

-Johnny Bench

The better a player is, the more often I'll be called to bust a slump. Bob Rotella's advice is to put things into perspective, dwell on the positive, look for something good to happen, and rededicate to the short game. I would add revisiting all of the Basic Skills. Other successful techniques in sports are focusing on body language, self-talk, and mantras.

Olympic track and field coach Mel Rosen regularly observes an athlete's body language before a meet. If the athlete hangs his head or shuffles his feet, Rosen will remind his pupil of his prior successes, infusing Rosen's belief into his student, and convincing the student to believe in himself and his ability to win the race. Focus upon your body language. In golf, slumping the shoulders or lowering the head dramatically influence posture, which can lead to poor mechanics as well as poor mental attitude. Good posture with head up, shoulders back, chest broad, and chin out can by itself break a player out of a slump.

Early in his tennis career, Pete Sampras regularly got caught up in negative tension and self-talk. As a pro, he took care to repeat positive phrases to himself during a match, such as, "I need to let go of that last point and stay focused on the present." If you have doubts about any shot your are about to hit, stop and reset. Take deep breaths, go through you preshot routine, stretch, do whatever you need to do to get negative thoughts and tension out of your body and mind. Many students will say after hitting a poor shot, "I knew I was going to do that." As a coach it baffles me why anyone would pull the trigger thinking they were going to execute poorly. There is no cost in stopping and resetting. That people regularly execute a shot without having properly prepared mentally goes against every notion of common sense. Ensure that you have positive sponsoring thoughts prior to execution, and don't execute a shot until you are positive of a positive outcome.

Finally, mantras are one of the most useful hypnotic tools in optimizing performance. Mantras can assist you to regain your center through the repetition of reciting a phrase or verse. Choose a mantra based upon your spiritual beliefs, or use the vision statement you developed through the exercises in the book. A mantra should be confident, powerful, and grounded. It should express a bedrock foundation of faith in your abilities. Some examples of successful mantras are: I am a confident, peaceful, powerful human being with all the abilities and knowledge necessary to execute this shot. When you have developed a mantra, repeat it over and over again to yourself, breathing slowly and deeply. Recite the mantra slowly, focusing on each syllable. After you have said it three times, begin your preshot routine. Reciting your mantra throughout a round will assist you with staying grounded and focused upon the present moment.

"It's easy for all of us to get too analytical in our approach to golf, and then we wind up taking twice as long to work our way out of a slump than if we'd just let it work itself out naturally."

-Larry Nelson

ACCELERATE YOUR PROCESS
LIVE NEXT TO THE HOLE

"We must accept finite disappointment, but we must never lose infinite hope."
-Martin Luther King, Jr.

In Jungian psychology there is a metaphor called The Shadow. The Shadow is represented by many things, and I like to simplify it by defining it as what we are in our worst moments. The Shadow is our fears, limitations, and anxieties all wrapped up in twine made of fear and insecurity. It may surface only occasionally or it may control a great many of your day-to-day activities. It definitely controls your game.

The Shadow shows up in your emotions, and illustrate the limits of your progress. Students often fail to improve because they get comfortable with their game, become complacent, and fail to repeat the routines that led to their mastery. This is a wonderful outcome for most teachers, as their livelihood is never in jeopardy. The problem isn't in the mechanics, but the student's unwillingness to improve beyond the limits of their emotional capacity for success and failure. Great students are never satisfied, and yet never become jaded or depressed by lack of immediate outcomes. I like to think that they live next to the hole. They are keenly aware of their abilities and limitations and they aren't afraid to explore WHY they're stuck on a particular shot our score. These students don't practice themselves out of the hole, they go into the hole.

Every student has a score that he hasn't broken. For some of my professional students, the number may be 68 or 69. They just can't seem to "break through." No matter how much they practice their short game, no matter how well they play, they always seem to wind up on a number that they are comfortable with. Often, I'll have these students play from the Forward, Senior, or Ladies tee just to see what happens. Almost invariably, students will shoot their number. They will hit the low number they tend toward no matter the course conditions or their level of commitment. After the round, I usually ask what happened, and the usual answer is, "I just didn't get the ball in the hole." Students always admit that they knew they might shoot a very low number, and that this got in the way. They had excitement, or nervousness, or, more likely, fear. What would it mean if they had shot 65, 64, 63? Or, if they had broken 80 for the first time? The truth is that most people are afraid of taking their game to the next level. It might mean more practice, more commitment, or a tremendous amount of disappointment if they broke their scoring record and could never repeat it.

A teacher once told me about Ellsworth and Emery Kolb, two brothers who spent the better part of a century photographing and exploring the Grand Canyon. Their filming spanned from 1903 to 1976, and included the first motion pictures of the canyon that were displayed and sent all over the world. If you ever tour the park, you can see the house where they lived out their lives. It is a small self-built structure on the edge of a thousand foot cliff. You can open a window and literally look straight down into the canyon. The metaphor is that the brothers lived on the edge of something unknown, and probably scary as hell. But they did it every day. They became accustomed and knowledge-able about the hole.

Choosing to live near the edge of our limitations and fears is quite different from constantly being pushed toward it. The closer you stay to the limit of your abilities as a golfer, or to your comfort zone as a person, the more rapid will be your growth.

Golfers who want to break their low score must get acquainted with the thoughts they have as they're approaching breaking the scoring barrier. One of my most successful students lowered his low score three strokes one season, and his scoring average by more than three, simply by being aware of the messages he was sending himself as he would regularly hit every fairway and every green. As soon as he heard himself saying, "Man, I've hit every one so far, I'm due to miss" or "If I make this, I'll shoot 62" he real-ized that he wasn't process oriented.

Living near the hole means having a constant and critical awareness of the thoughts (and particularly fears) that creep into your mind as you perform both poorly and opti-mally. Students stall because they are not honest and aware about what is going on internally. You cannot grow beyond and master what you are not aware of. Your emotions show you the limits of your growth in life and golf. If you do nothing, or if you choose to accept where you are, you are solidifying the patterns that gave rise to your present per-formance. And you will likely only repeat the process, not move beyond it.

DRILL:

1. List everything you avoid
(chores, in-laws, phobias, courses, course conditions).

2. Look at these avoidances though the eyes of someone who knows and loves you.   What would he see?

3. If you gave this person permission to change anything in your life that would limit or destroy these avoidances, what would he do?

4. Consider for a moment why you aren't doing these things.

5. Resolve to sit with your discomfort about the changes you need to make to stop the avoidances. You're not committing to doing anything, just sitting with your resistances. Do this for at least five minutes at a time. Time yourself. Notice the way your mind wanders. Restart the exercise as many times as you need until you can sit with your discomfort for at least five minutes.

6. Notice the power of your resistance. This is what holds you back. The closer you come to the edges, the nearer you live to them, and the more aware you are of their presence, the faster your process will accelerate. You don't have to do

anything. Just be aware of it.

7. Never stop doing this drill. Ever.

> "If you don't pay attention to the messages of your emotions, don't worry. Another message will come."
> -Gary Zukov

"The journey of a thousand miles must
begin with a single step."

Lau-Tsu

IMAGERY & VISIONING

What is behind your eyes is more important than what
is in front of them.

-Dr. Mac Powell

The sensory system is the only mechanism you have to evaluate the world around you. We learn through our senses,
and based upon the data we receive, form images of the
world around us. Imagery is using our visual (seeing),
auditory (hearing and balance), and kinesthetic (touching
and feeling) abilities in union to optimize performance.

Sports Psychologist Bob Rotella teaches that golf is a game
of confidence, played with the eyes. What you see you create. This is echoed time and time again in Tiger Woods'
How I Play Golf. Tiger continually asserts that envisioning
a shot is the critical component in golf performance.
However, I would like to assert that visioning is only part of
the equation. Using all of your senses will bring the "picture" more clearly into focus and create a stronger mental
connection to the swing you want to perform.

Ben Hogan would repeatedly play a round of golf in his
mind to improve his performance in tournament play.
Mary Decker, an Olympic runner in the 1984 games, led
until falling in her final heat. Of her loss, she said, "I didn't
visualize myself finishing the race." Studies have found
that performance can regularly be enhanced without physical practice, and that intensely visualizing optimal outcomes substantially increases the probability they will

occur.

Many of my students state that they have a difficulty visualizing completely, yet have little difficulty when I ask them to recall their wedding day, the birth of a child, or a death of someone close to them. Recalling joyous or traumatic events demonstrates that everyone can learn to visualize with intense focus. What is required is finding "intensity in the minutia," to dramatize the mundane. In golf, you must visualize intensely. See yourself finishing a shot and the ball going in the hole or landing close to the pin. Always feel how the shot felt at impact and how you felt as the ball was soaring in the air. Complete visualization requires incorporation of all of your senses and the completion of the desired outcomes.

DRILL:

1. Reward yourself for your mental accomplishments...not your score. Stop keeping track of your strokes. Score yourself on how well you were able to visualize completely before you executed your shot. Don't score the result. Score your mental preparation from 1-100 on each hole and track your progress between rounds. Reward improvement!

2. Look from the back of your eyes. One of the most important lessons I learned in my training is that we are capable of looking from different perspectives. Most people spend their lives on edge, wide-eyed, and looking outward at their

surroundings, trying to manipulate or control. When at peace, however, we tend to look as though from the back of our eyes. Our eye muscles relax and we become aware of how we SEE our surroundings. Put differently, we are able to step back and see our environment from a third-person perspective. Become aware of whether you are looking from the front of your eyes or the back of your eyes, and practice drawing back your focus. By doing so, your ability to visualize optimal outcomes will expand.

"I never hit a shot, even in practice, without having a very sharp, in-focus picture of it in my mind"
-Jack Nicklaus

THE PRESHOT ROUTINE

80% of the shot occurs before the backswing begins.

Mastery of the game of golf requires a mastery of the preshot routine, which won't be possible until you've mastered all of the Basic Skills. However, the technique of any solid preshot routine must include at least all of the following. As you begin to retool your game, remember that the preshot routine is the foundation upon which your game is built. Have you built yours on the sand, on the rocks, or on a level foundation of solid earth?

Evaluation:

Evaluate the lie, the wind, the condition of the ground around the ball, the slope of the ground, and the receptiveness of the target.

Evaluate your own inner process. Is your body tired, elevated, flexible, relaxed, upset, or anxious?

What are the risk-reward benefits of the possible shots you might execute? What shots has the course architect foreseen and where are the "no miss zones" (bunkers, out of bounds, short side of greens, and chipping areas)

Decision:

Decide on a target. Focus on the smallest possible

point. A blade of grass or a part of a leaf would be ideal.

Decide on the shot shape, trajectory, and begin to feel what the shot would feel like during execution.

Visualize that outcome. From completion to beginning if possible, and always in real time.

Execution:

Holding your eyes to the target, address the ball with your feet together. Make sure the ball is in the proper position in your stance.

Find the target with your eyes.

Align your club.

Separate your feet the proper width.

Find the target with your eyes.

Check for tension in your body and release it as necessary.

Take a slow breath.

Find the target in your mind's eye.

Begin the swing.

Finish the swing to the target.

Hold your finish on the target.

See the ball landing and finishing on the target.

Rules regarding pace of play dictate that this process take only ninety seconds. It probably took you longer than that just to review the synopsis of what has to occur prior to the execution and completion of a shot. Mastering the preshot routine requires all of these activities to take place unconsciously. Always in order and never rushed or hurried. Confidence requires knowing what will happen before the ball is struck. You wouldn't want to take a different swing to every shot. Why would you take a different mental approach? If your preshot routine is inconsistent, expect your shots to be inconsistent as well.

Master the preshot routine by reviewing the Basic Skills, incorporating them into your practice and play, and trusting them under pressure.

3 FOOT TOSSES

> "Nothing is particularly hard if you divide it into small jobs."
>
> -Henry Ford

The dynasty of the Joe Montana-Bill Walsh San Francisco 49ers is not their four Super Bowl rings, but their demonstration that a well-executed game plan based upon controlled balanced movement is superior to desperate low-percentage passing. Golfers would benefit from employing this concept in their own games. Too many golfers try to make up strokes or manufacture scoring by swinging for the fences and going for inaccessible pins rather than maintaining strategic position and playing shots that are likely to lead to success. The odds of a mid-handicapper making a twenty-foot putt are substantially greater than a mid-handicapper hitting a three hundred yard drive in the fairway, driving a green, or reaching a par-five in two. If you have ever watched touring professionals, you know that the key to scoring is in their ability to chip-in or pitch it close. Improving ball striking and driving distance will not lead to the kind of improvement that most golfers seek. Tiger Woods repeatedly credits his success to scrambling, not driving distance. If you want to improve scoring, formulate a well-executed game plan based upon balanced movement and ball control.

One of the best lessons I learned in my training had nothing to do, or so it seemed, with psychology or sports performance. A group of graduate students was divided into two teams and given an assignment: beat the other group in a game of ring toss. Each of the teams had three rings to toss around pegs scattered three feet away, six feet away, nine feet away, and twelve feet away. One point was given for a three-foot toss, two points for a six foot toss, three points for a nine foot toss, and five points for a twelve-foot toss. As each of us got up to throw our rings, it became readily apparent that the six, nine, and twelve foot tosses were long shots. Out of a hundred throws, maybe three or four landed on the farther pegs. However, the three-foot tosses were slam dunks. We could just bend over at the waist and lay the rings over the peg for a point. At the end of the assignment, the totals were added, and the team that took the most three-foot tosses won. Period. I've replicated the experiment in clinics. The result is always the same. I think of it like this. The longer throws are like Hail Marys, and you only throw a Hail Mary if you're desperate. Here's how to not get desperate in golf.

Any task can be divided into a set of three-foot tosses. Any task. I have worked with many clients who wanted seemingly impossible things given their circumstances: opening a business, losing over one hundred pounds, or going to medical school for example. Although the tasks seemed daunting, like a Hail Mary unlikely to be completed, when broken down into a series of steps (going to pick up an application to a university, completing the application, submitting the application, registering for classes, and so on) anything becomes doable.

It is impossible to go from a 20 handicapper to a professional simply by thinking "it's going to happen." However, if you break the process into steps, into a series of three-foot tosses, and support your goals by daily with physical, emotional, mental, and physical activities that bring you closer to your destination, any feat is achievable.

The most effective mechanism to exercise the three-foot toss is a 30-Day Action Plan. The Plan will assist you with creating measurable and repeatable steps that will lead you toward your trajectory. Commit to at least one action in each category and track your progress daily.

Directions:

When you have committed to a trajectory you would like to take, brainstorm on the tiniest steps you can take toward that trajectory. Divide the steps into the following areas, and commit to taking at least one measurable step from each category daily.

Physical-Actions you take with your body in the physical world: going to the gym, swimming 20 minutes, breathing exercises, and hitting balls at the range are examples.

Mental-Actions you take primarily for or with your mind: reading a book, playing a practice round in your mind, reviewing your performance from a previous round, visualization.

Emotional-Actions you take to facilitate the expression or

healing of emotions: writing a feeling list, journaling about feelings, meditating on the sensations in your body and connecting them to feelings, telling others how you feel (rather than what you think).

Spiritual-Actions you take to facilitate spiritual growth: going to church, praying, meditating, doing volunteer work, giving to others, thanking the universe for your life and possessions.

30 DAY ACTION PLAN

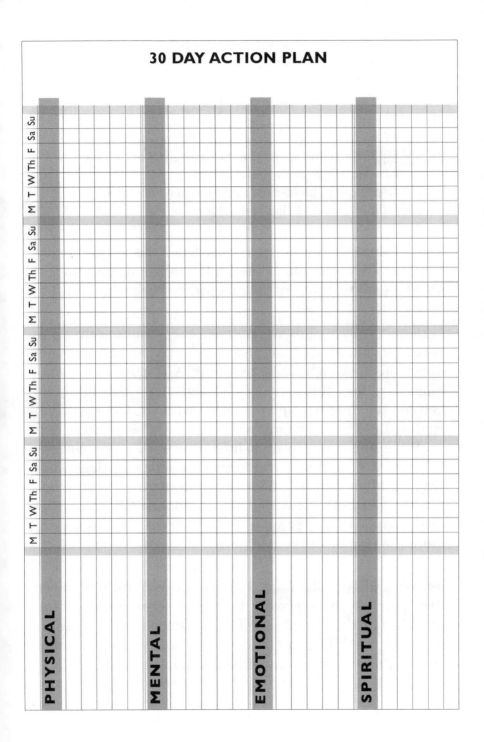

REFRAMING

"As every man had ever a point of pride that was not injurious to him, so no man had ever a defect that was not somewhere made useful to him...
Every man in his lifetime needs to thank his faults."
                                                    -Ralph Waldo Emerson

The wisdom of reframing comes from the adage "Every cloud has a silver lining," and adds to it a deeper understanding of the power of language upon performance.

Perhaps the best golfing example of the power of reframing is Ben Hogan. Hogan was an average player by all accounts during his first eight years on the PGA Tour. Despite winning only one tournament between 1931 and 1939, he became the dominant player in the world at the age of 32, leading the Tour in winnings five times between 1940 and 1948, an amazing accomplishment given that his success followed a near fatal car accident in which his legs were crushed after throwing his body onto his wife to save her life. Hogan used his tragedy as an opportunity to rededicate himself to the game and went on to win twenty-six more times, nine of them majors.

As you evaluate situations and make decisions, remember that your psyche responds to your interpretation of the stimuli, not the stimuli itself. The human mind takes in only one one-billionth (1/1,000,000,000) of the available stimuli that the environment offers. It interprets the selected stimuli and determines how you respond. How you interpret your performance drastically affects future outcomes. Do you see a missed chip as an opportunity to show off your putting? Do you see a drive into the rough as an opportunity to refocus your mind, to be thankful your bad shots are behind you or do you see your mistakes as an omen of forthcoming failures?

Be aware of the opportunities in "bad shots" or missed putts. The alternative is despair or resignation, neither of which has a produced major championships.

Two of my favorite players are Peter Thompson and Gary Player. Thompson was without doubt the greatest match play player of his generation. Not the longest hitter, he would regularly "let" his opponent out drive him, allowing his opponent to think he had the advantage. Thompson would then knock down pins with laser-like approach shots. This regularly wore down opponents and energized Thompson. He turned his lack of length into a strength and captured five British Opens. Gary Player, quite similarly, would rave about how he loved slow greens, that slow greens favored his style of play, and that he always felt he was going to win on slow greens. The following week he would be singing the praises of fast greens, how his putting stroke favored the touch required on fast greens, and by all means, the faster the better. No matter the condition, Gary found a way to find them to his liking. By reframing what other players saw as difficulties, Player entered tournaments with an advantage, helping him to secure nine major championships and the career grand slam at the age of 29.

Reframe your catastrophes as challenges and your limitations as opportunities. Every time you feel frustration, remember that your energy can be served by directing it toward positive purposes. Dedicate yourself to seeing the opportunity in every situation: slow greens, fast greens, long drives, or being thirty yards behind an opponent in the fairway.

> "To be thrown upon one's own resources is to be cast into the very lap of fortune, for our faculties then undergo a development and display of energy of which they were previously unsusceptible."
> -Benjamin Franklin

THE POWER OF THE PRESENT

"The present is the point at which time touches eternity."

-C.S. Lewis

The way to form consistent success is to become process oriented. In 2004, Davis Love III rose to near the top of PGA Tour putting statistics after spending much of his career among the Tour's most mediocre. Love credited his success to a method of "Getting into the Process," employed by one of the Tour's most consistently excellent putters, Brad Faxon.

Getting into the Process is more than performing a consistent pre-shot routine. It is an expression of the notion that the past is an endless stream of possibilities gone by, and the future is an endless stream of possibilities yet to occur. The present differs from the past and future in that it is the only one that we experience. Being in The Zone is a metaphor for the sensation of experiencing all possibilities and unconsciously choosing and executing the most optimal from among them. You should plan and practice with your conscious mind so as to allow your unconscious mind to perform during a round of golf. Because sustaining complete mental focus over the course of a 4 _ hour round is next to impossible, a solid pre-shot routine that recognizes the importance of Getting into the Process allows a golfer to focus his mind for the less than 4 to 5 minutes needed to begin and complete the swings in a round. Being Present Moment Aware or Getting into the Process is essential to find the required balance between concentration and detachment.

DRILL:

1. Think of an intimidating Par 3 with a long carry over water or a downhill five foot right-breaking putt on 18 to shoot 79. Notice any tension in your chest, forearms, back, or neck. With that tension, are you likely to carry the water or hit the putt firm and center-cut? Now try the following breathing exercise.

2. Focus on your breathing. Notice the pace, depth, and quality of the breath passing in and out of your lungs. Is your breathing becoming faster or slower as you notice its rhythm?

3. Take a long deep inhalation through both nostrils, holding the breath with the deepest portion of your diaphragm for a full second before slowly and evenly allowing the breath to escape through your mouth. Repeat this three times, filling your lungs to 100% capacity. Notice any sensations in your body. Are you agitated or nervous, frightened, or incredulous? Repeat the exercise as necessary to achieve a state of deep calm awareness. This is the state from which your best golf will blossom.

4. Once you've completed the breathing exercise,
try visualizing the long carry over water or hard-breaking

putt again. Notice how easy it is to see yourself making the putt or carrying the ball high over the water and landing it softly near the pin.

Success requires planting the correct positive thought into your consciousness at the moment prior execution. If your mind is racing, fumbling through past misses, worrying about the line or the lie, or focused upon your score rather than executing the shot at hand, you run the risk of planting a "bad seed" prior to the moment of execution. Becoming present focused through an awareness of your breathing slows down the thought process, giving you greater control and predictability over the thoughts you will drop into your unconscious prior to the moment of execution.

> "Now or never! You must live in the present, launch yourself on every wave, find your eternity in each moment."
>
> -Henry David Thoreau

RULES AND STRATEGY

"Did you ever observe to whom the accidents happen?
Chance favors only the prepared mind."
-Louis Pasteur

One of the things I find most interesting about working with students is the predictability of the concern after an initial consultation: "I'm hitting the ball better, putting great, am target conscious, but I'm not scoring like I feel I should."

The reason is course management. Ben Hogan, the master of dissecting a course, would decide where he was going to hit the ball days or weeks ahead. His strategy wasn't formulated under pressure, or at the whim of streaks or missed opportunities. Course management is an acknowledgement, well in advance of stepping to the tee, of our strengths and limitations.

Every course has idiosyncrasies that must be acknowledged, and every golfer has tendencies that must be accounted for and incorporated into a game plan. Here are some simple rules that may be common knowledge, but which are rarely practiced in Sunday foursomes. They are rules because there are no exceptions. These will lead to success 99.9% of the time over capricious, careless and/or overaggressive or defensive decision-making.

1. Always play to the middle of greens and fairways unless you have a wedge in your hand. Be aggressive inside 100

yards.

2. Always incorporate the shot you bring from the practice tee. If you were hitting a fade, play the fade. On the tee box, stand to the right side and aim to the left center of the fairway. Accept the swing you bring to the course.

3. Always putt the ball in or past the hole. Putts that don't get to the hole don't go in.

4. Always be aware of your conscious thoughts and bodily sensations. If you have negative or destructive thoughts or feelings, step away from a shot.

5. Always use your preshot routine. Never waver.

6. Always trust your eyes. Visualize your shot and trust that your body will compensate for any mechanical imperfections. Never carry a mechanical thought to the ball.

7. Always have fun. Anger, frustration, anxiety, jealousy, and the expression of these emotions will destroy your game. If you hope to improve, it is wiser to leave the course than to allow these emotions to control you in practice or play.

8. Always carry a learning orientation to the course and try your best to stay in the moment, working only on the shot at hand.

9. Always accept what has happened and always see the next shot as an opportunity to express your mastery of the game.

10. Never allow your score to affect your play or mood. The easiest way to do this is to not keep score. Track only your ability to stay in the moment and score yourself in relation to what it would be like to be completely aware of the present and all its possibilities.

These rules will optimize performance. Make all of your decisions before you set foot on the golf course. The more you are able to leave your conscious mind behind, the truer your shots will be.

Finally, I like to substitute the word practice with preparation. Practice often implies mindless ball-beating. Decide to prepare for your next event, or next foursome ahead of time. Devise a schedule to work on your game (devoting at least 50% of the time to your short game) and decide what mindset you will carry with you before you arrive at the practice green, range, or first tee.

Keep these rules handy when you practice and play until you can dutifully recall them under pressure. Proper strategy can overcome moments of poor execution..

"I shall prepare myself. Someday my chance will come."
-Abraham Lincoln

RULES AND STRATEGY II

"If I had cleared the trees and drove the green, it would've been a great shot."

-Sam Snead

There are no more disturbing words in golf than "should" and "would." They imply that what has occurred is not the perfect result of what preceded. If a putt missed off to the right it rolled off because there was too much break, too little speed, or that the putt was off line from the beginning. Rules and Strategy II requires that you begin with a perfect game plan and execute it to the best of your ability. This does not mean that your plan will be executed perfectly. Shots will go astray, putts will not drop. A perfectly executed round requires complete acceptance over past shots and a centered present moment awareness of the shot at hand.

In her audio-book Golf in the Zone, Marcia Reynolds states that playing good golf requires that you stop convincing yourself or others and begin to listen and accept your situation as it is. If you hit a drive 220 yards on the first hole and need a carry of 250 yards over a bunker on the second hole, play away from the bunkers! This may seem like common sense, but golfers seem to have an innate ability to lose this valuable wisdom during a round. If you want to take a risk, take it with a wedge in your hand. With any other club, aim for the fairway or middle of the green.

Tiger Woods has often said that he plays away from dangerous zones on the golf course. He plays the shot he brings to the course, but never aims over water, trees, or out of bounds unless absolutely necessary. Bruce Litzcke is a player who has played world-class golf for decades without being able to hit a draw. He stands on the left side of the tee box, aims down the left side, and consistently fades the ball into the fairway. On holes that require a left to right shot he uses a 3-wood, lays up, and more times than not, makes a par.

These decisions are difficult to make under the pressure of tournament play, or while being ribbed by your playing partners. The best time to make these strategic choices is during your mental preparation before a round. Most world-class golfers have learned to play the course in their mind, visualize the outcomes, and make important decisions ahead of time, and focus on reacting to shots as they happen.

Rules and Strategy II is about making perfect decisions before stepping onto the golf course. If you make your target and shot decisions ahead of time, it will be easier to focus and perform

Begin to see your game being played out ahead of time. Golfer's greatest mistakes are made when players attempt shots they don't have consistently execute in practice. The following drill will assist you in preparing a perfect plan for an approaching round.

DRILL:

Review the Basic Skill: Imagery and Visioning and begin to prepare well ahead of your round so that you can begin to unconsciously react to shots. If your conscious mind carries thoughts of swing plane, tempo, target, takeaway, and breathing, you are unlikely to succeed. You must learn to get out of your own way and this requires preparation.

1. Think of the last competitive round you played and the course where it took place. Without reviewing your performance, recall the course and the shots that the course architect intended you to play.

2. Play the course in your mind, remembering the Rules and Strategies discussed in this book. Aim for the center of the fairway, for the center of greens. Feel yourself executing each shot completely, staying in the present moment. Observe yourself effortlessly scoring on each hole. Complete the entire round before moving to the next step.

3. What did it feel like in your visioning to play the course from the middle of the fairway, from attacking only pins with a wedge? If you noticed an absence of tension, it is because golf is a different game when played with proper strategy. Learn to take this vision with you on the golf course, focusing only one shot at a time, seeing and feeling the shots more easily because you have done your decision-making well before you step on the course.

Ben Hogan was chided for saying that he didn't understand why most people didn't shoot par. Approach golf with

Hogan's preparation, and par becomes a realistic goal for players of all abilities.

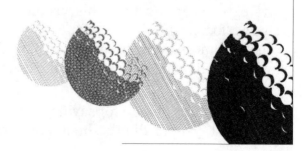

SKILLS FOR
MASTERY

ARTISTRY - SILENCING THE INNER CRITIC

"Every child is an artist. The problem is to remain an artist once he grows up."
-Pablo Picasso

In her book on creative recovery, The Artist's Way, Julia Cameron teaches students that life can be a creative endeavor, offering that through golf, for instance, we can find passion, vitality, and fulfillment. The common barrier to this transformation is the Inner Critic. It is the voice that tells you that you should have made a putt or that you'll never reach your golfing potential. It is the voice that convinces you to hit the shorter club so that you won't look weak, or to go for a pin placement because playing safe is for losers. It is your ego, a dangerous element in golf if not understood and accorded a place in your psyche that can facilitate mastery.

Cameron's book is an excellent resource to tap into the joy of creativity. For our purposes, it's important to understand our own inner dialogue and how critical messages impact our performance. The following drill is an introduction to this process and I encourage you to visit Cameron's work more thoroughly at some point in your development.

DRILL:

1. If you haven't already done so, begin a daily journal. I found great resistance in performing this task, but was reminded of something that Eleanor Roosevelt said: "We must do the things we think we cannot." I often rephrase this for clients as "We must do the things that we most don't want to do." There is great benefit from journaling, and I recommend either making a daily journal out of durable artistic material or writing Morning Pages and Evening Pages, placing the pages in an envelope, sealing and dating the envelope, and putting it away somewhere that you can retrieve them months or years ahead. The key to journaling is to write freely and not to censor yourself.

2. Complete the Vision, Energy Drains, and Barriers worksheets in the workbook. The barriers and energy drains we create, or refuse to move beyond, are a manifestation of our Inner Critic.

3. What is the Inner Critic saying by blocking you in a particular way? The best way to understand your Inner Critic is to dialogue with it. Begin to incorporate a question and answer session in your journaling. Ask open-ended questions that allow your Inner Critic to speak. It has something valuable to say, and your "mistakes" on the golf course are the not-so-subtle messages it has been sending to you.

4. Make peace with your Inner Critic so that will no longer surface on the golf course. This requires a true reckoning. Allow your Inner Critic to express what he or she has to say

in your journaling. Again, it will be valuable. If you fail to listen effectively, your Inner Critic will have no choice but to continue to thwart you in order to gain your attention. Once the Inner Critic has been heard, you may gently thank it and dismiss it, reminding it that it is valuable and will continue to be a part of your journaling sessions, but that it no longer has a purpose on the course.

Gaining the alliance of your Inner Critic allows the Inner Artist to come forward. Instead of practicing to stave off failure, prepare to embrace success.

THE FOUR SELVES

"If you wish to travel far and fast, travel light. Take off all your envies, jealousies, unforgiveness, selfishness and fears."

-Glenn Clark

Although the Types offer insight into the behaviors and propensities of our character, the deeper more authentic questions must address the bigger notion of Self. There are Four Selves of which we must be aware, and a fifth, or Authentic Self, which lends to more metaphysical or spiritual discussions. The Four Selves are: The Past Self, The Present Self, The Ideal Self, and The Self as Others See You. Each Type will exhibit these Selves in different ways. In fact, the unique expression of these Selves is more dependent upon your upbringing and circumstances than the overall pattern of your personality.

The reason I said earlier that you must be aware of these is that if you are not aware of them, they are likely to surreptitiously undo your best efforts. The Four Selves have different needs, different methods, and different histories, but they are equally dangerous enemies and allies.

The Past Self for many is what they were, what they had, and what they did. Unfortunately, the Past Self tends to become either "half empty" or "half full" and stays that way throughout the course of our lives. This is one reason why people who are generally optimistic tend to repeat positive outcomes. Their Past Self wills them to repeat their patterns. Unfortunately, those with Past Selves that see the glass as "half empty" tend to see the past as a series of opportunistic failures. This wouldn't be so bad if the Past Self didn't have such a close allegiance to the Present Self, which is how we see ourselves, what we are, and who we are in the present moment. Psychologist Martin Seligman studied the difference between optimists, pessimists, and realists and found that optimists tend to have more consistently successful outcomes, often because they did not believe that their past poor performances have nothing to do with their present or future performance. For most people, the Past Self is informing the Present Self, presenting images and sensations about what we did the last time, or the last ten times. Getting on a hot streak or breaking a pattern requires that you differentiate the Past Self from the Present Self. If the Present Self is allowed to operate, to react to the stimuli in front of it, you have a chance at optimal performance. If your Past Self is in any way informs your Present Self with a half empty orientation, it will be difficult to break patterns or obtain optimal performance.

The Ideal Self is in many ways the solution to the problem of poor performance. It has been said that the Ideal Self is what you are or would like to be "in your best moments." Students are often extremely skilled at willing themselves to optimal performance in the short term, and this is frequently accomplished by precise goal setting and actually SEEING success in advance of its happening. My own practice of using the Ideal Self is a balance of two voices in my head: the Ideal Self (who I am in my best moments) and the

Past Self (in my case a glass half full voice reminding me of my shortcomings). These two elements of self are passionate spokespersons for particular types of outcomes. The Ideal Self reminds me that I am capable of knocking down pins; the Past Self reminds me that I often get stuck under the lips of bunkers when I get greedy; the Present Self listens quietly most of the time and tries to make the best decision possible. The honest truth is that optimal performance comes from getting the Ideal Self and the Past Self to quietly allow the Present Self to stay in the moment, judge shotmaking, and get the ball in the hole. That's why Chevy Chase does the "nananana" thing in Caddyshack while he's holing putts from all over the green. Try it sometime. He's really blocking out the Ideal and Past selves. The sound he is making drowns them out, and consequently, his Present Self gets to do what it does best. Experience and execute. See ball, hit ball.

And here enters the Self as Others See You. Right now, this aspect of you is thinking, "I'm not doing that. Only a crazy person would go to the practice green and do that. What would people think? Maybe if no one was around though, I might." You are predictable because of the Self as Others See You. You do what you think you are supposed to do; you perform the role others want from you; you repeat the same phrases and behaviors because they are comfortable, and because you and others expect you to repeat them. You are predictable. Very predictable. Breaking through performance barriers requires you to adjust the Self as Others See You. I honestly believe this aspect is the easiest to manipulate in the short-term, but the hardest to change in the long term. In reality, all you have to do is tell other people that you're changing. "Hey world, I am now going to be a world class golfer!" You tell the world, and see who listens. The people who say, "That's awesome, how can I support you?" are the people you keep and see regularly. People who reinforce your doubts may say: "Are you good enough?," "How will you have time with all the work you have?," "What does your wife/husband/partner say about that?," " Can you afford it?," and/or "Are you sure this is what you want to do?." These people are consciously or unconsciously forming an alliance with your Past Self to ensure that you remain as you were. And this is one of the promises I can make: If you allow others, whether through their words, attitudes or behaviors, to influence how you think of yourself, you will fall short. Period. This works for positive and negative influences. Golf is an inner game. You will stand alone on the course and you must learn to rely upon yourself.

Start now. Decide what you will be. Align the Ideal and Past Selves. Convince the Self as Others See You that you will only listen and associate with those who are supportive, and let the Present Self run the show. You are a capable individual, but the act of allowing others to chip away at who you are and what you want is more damaging than any personal tragedy, no matter how catastrophic. Never ALLOW anyone to control what is important to you, how you think, or how you perform. You are the ultimate decision maker. Remember that. You will need that determination to be a great player.

STORY TELLING

"The hero ventures forth from the world of common day into a region of supernatural wonder: fabulous forces are there encountered and a decisive victory is won: the hero comes back from this mysterious adventure with the power to bestow boons on his fellow man."

-Joseph Campbell, Hero with a Thousand Faces

What is the story of your life? All lives follow a story, and many peoples' stories share similar plot points. Psychologist Carl Jung labeled these common plots archetypes: characters, themes, and images that present themselves in the myths and literary works of almost all worldwide cultures. Some of our culture's more well-known archetypes can be found in the same film, Star Wars: Luke Skywalker was the hero or savior, Darth Vader the shadow or transformed evil, the Emperor represented death, Obi-Won Kenobi represented the mentor, Princess Leia the love interest or Madonna, Han Solo the rival or rebel, and C3-PO and R2-D2 served as the comic relief. The Star Wars series revolves the archetypal themes of good versus evil, the growth and acceptance of self, overcoming family or interpersonal secrets, and the triumph of the self over adversity.

Our individual life stories surface in our hopes and dreams. Acknowledging theses stories and learning from the archetypal messages can assist us overcoming our limitations. As golfers, we play out our stories on the course, particularly during times of stress. Are we trying to attain perfection on the golf course in order to compensate for other deficient areas of our lives? Are we fierce competitors trying to destroy our opponents or are we helpers, constantly more concerned about the games of the people around us, quick to compliment but slow to appreciate our own good fortune?

Recognizing the stories you are replaying can assist you in growing as a golfer and a person.

DRILL:

1. Review your Vision Statement. Review the following list of golf archetypes and identify your quest from the list below. Just pick one. You can always review this material later, but choose one quest for now.

2. Sample Quests

> The Innocent Quest. The object tof the Innocent Quest is to remain in safety or ignorance. Often the person is optimistic and trusting, but afraid to seek his own limitations. If a personal challenge is presented, the innocent will seek outside assistance or rescue from the challenge. Types associated with this quest are Advisors, Mystics, Skeptics, and Peacemakers.

> The Warrior Quest. The warrior's overt objective is victory, though he is always cautious of being exploit-

ed by those around him. The warrior's life task is to process and FEEL, but he is vulnerable to his own misgivings about what will happen if he indulges his feelings. Types associated with this quest are Crusaders, Achievers, and Mavericks.

The Caregiver Quest. Though the caregiver's virtues are compassion and generosity, he often fears that he is too selfish. The caregiver must overcome his shadow and indulge his selfishness enough to care for himself, ultimately reconciling his guilt over the seeming contradiction. The Type most associated with this quest is the Advisor.

The Lover Quest. The lover hopes to find bliss and brings passion and commitment to all endeavors. Although he fears the loss of love, the lover must face the experience of that likely possibility with acceptance and grace. Peacemakers often find themselves reenacting this quest, as do Mystics and Jokers.

The Sage Quest. The sage's quest is to find truth and transcend it. While he seeks enlightenment, he fears deception, and must overcome his reliance upon the intellect. The Type associated with this quest is the Thinker.

The Fool Quest. The fool enjoys life for its own sake, and is terrified of death and boredom. The fool's task is to trust the process of becoming and to accept his own eccentricity and possible conformity in the same breath. The Type most associated with this quest is the

Joker.

3. Spend a moment thinking about your story or quest and whether this is the archetype you would like to continue manifesting. What are the benefits and what are the obstacles of this quest? What do you get out of replaying this story?

4. What are the barriers and Energy Drains typically associated with this quest? List them in new Energy Drains Worksheets.

5. Develop at least four action steps, one each at the Mental, Emotional, Physical, and Spiritual level, and monitor your progress with a new 30-Day Action Plan.

6. Revisit this list of archetypes weekly, thinking about your own, as well as the archetypes and quests of the people you encounter on the course.

7. Stay committed to your dreams through your 30-Day Action Plan.

> "When Jung, in his eighties, was discussing at his house the process of becoming conscious with a group of young psychiatrists...he ended with the surprising words: And then you have to learn to become decently unconscious."
>
> -Aniela Jaffe

MASTERING SHORT-TERM MEMORY

"The palest ink is better than the best memory."
-Chinese Proverb

The mind is a tremendously predictable tool if you know how it works. The average person's mind can hold only three or four thoughts in its short-term memory at a time. This means you can only be thinking of a few things at once. My students quickly realize that if you're thinking about how many greens you've hit, how many putts you've made, what your score is going to be, or what it might mean if you break your scoring record, there is no room for Preshot Routine, Target, and Execution. Committing to the same thoughts, as well as the same swing mechanics, prevents your fears, insecurities, and doubts from adversely affecting your execution.

Program your short-term memory by committing to hold the same three or four thoughts in your mind each time you approach the ball. These four sponsoring thoughts should ideally be target, rhythm, and tempo. If you hold these thoughts firmly in your short-term memory, it is impossible for stray thoughts to enter. You only have room for three or four, so ensure they are consistent and positive, and improved outcomes are guaranteed.

YOU ARE NOT YOUR SCORES

"A man of character finds a special attractiveness in difficulty, since it is only by coming to grips with difficulty that he can realize his potentialities."
-Charles de Gaulle

You Are Not Your Scores is the hardest lesson for most golfers to accept. It strikes a similar vein as you are not your work, possessions, or friends. The cumulative experiences of your life and your own potentials are limitless and unabashedly unique.

There is no single event in your life, nor any phrase or accomplishment that could ever capture even a significant portion of who you are, and yet, people often measure themselves against a standard of play in a game. The game consumes them because they feel that it is the most important thing to them. To them, golf represents a particular frustration or barrier, or even still, a success, a fleeting moment of greatness and grandeur. I would like to suggest that while golf is a mirror to your uniqueness, to your story, it will never be you or your story. Golf is a tool, a metaphor, and opportunity to uncover new information.

Golf is an experience that assists you in connecting with what is under the surface. Behind the mask of the persona is who you are in your finest moments. It is unlikely that anyone truly knows this Authentic Self. It is unlikely that you know the Authentic Self well. This is probably because, like me, you were rewarded for obedience, conformity, and loyalty to a particular set of ideas and behaviors: Smile. Stand up straight. Come here. Do that. Eat this. You don't get any dessert if you don't.... and so on. Your Authentic Self is underneath the programmed responses. In some instances, you may feel your Authentic Self trying to speak, but the words may seem too harsh, too true. You may experience tension because what you really want to say does not conform with what you are expected to say or do.

Golf is a mirror of this process in Western culture. We convince ourselves of what should happen and become disappointed when it does not. When our expectations aren't fulfilled, instead of asking ourselves why we expected so-and-so to happen and learning from the limitations of what we perceived, we begin blaming ourselves, others, situations, and things.

We have become entangled in our own false expectations. Should is a dangerous word. Expecting a particular outcome, that the ball will go in the fairway, that a putt will drop, that a raise or a promotion will be bestowed, can easily lead to disappointment, which in turn, can lead to feelings of failure, inadequacy, shame, resentment, anger, guilt, and so on. The game is merely an opportunity for learning; missing a putt signals that we didn't read enough break, that we needed to rededicate ourselves to the short game, take a lesson, and/or practice more. Doesn't that sound simple? And yet, I find that 99.9% of the time people do not see that message. They see a missed putt as a product of unfair green conditions, a putter that won't keep the ball on line, or a ball that isn't perfectly balanced. Their unfulfilled expectations often carry over to the next tee, next fairway, next green. Aren't they entitled to a bit of luck? Shouldn't a few of the breaks go their way? When they don't, they can be unpleasant competitors or playing partners.

Golf doesn't keep track of missed opportunities. You must hit the next shot planning to execute it precisely, pouring yourself into the shot such that you have no doubt. If you do not, you leave the door open to fear and insecurity, both of which have the powerful ability to alter mechanics and send shots astray.

Remember to view success and failures as learning opportunities-performance is a reflection of a process, not of worth.

"What is behind your eyes is more important than what is in front of them"

Dr. Mac Powell

WESTERN PRACTICE, EASTERN PERFORMANCE

"The swing is never learned. It is remembered."
-Steven Pressfield, The Legend of Baggar Vance: A
Novel of Golf and the Game of Life

Embedded in the process of the Inner Game is the notion that we should practice in a Western Way and perform in an Eastern Way. Practice requires diligence, critical evaluation, and commitment to the mechanics of the process. Performance requires detachment, stillness of mind, and observance of the process.

In Zen in the Art of Archery, Daisetz Suzuki teaches that the way of perfection in archery is through "right mind", or the oneness of the archer, the bow, the arrow, and the target. Golf is no different. Right mind can't be accomplished by beating balls or reading books. It requires a mastery of the mechanics, whatever your own unique mechanics might be, and a deep understanding of how to access the present moment, the feeling of oneness, or The Zone.

Westerners are work-a-holics, shop-a-holics, addicts, and pleasure seekers. They are driven to succeed, and often believe that hard work will overcome all limitations. This is an attitude that believes that "If I don't do it, it won't get done." These are typical "grinder" values, and grinders often practice harder than everyone else. I admire grinders, and have been known to encourage the practice among my students. However, grinding has drawbacks. In a round, I don't encourage constant intense devoted attention any more than I encourage a willy-nilly approach to the game. Research on sports performance has found that the optimal attitude for athletes is one that allows for momentary ups and downs. Not mood swings, but also not constant intense focus. Players who "play angry" or "play without emotion" are both at a disadvantage compared to a player who allows himself to be flexible with his emotions on the course.

Students that have a passion for practice, who stay on the range past sunset, repeatedly hitting into trouble just to get out of it, wearing gloves and grips thin, are inspiring professionally. However, these students will stall if they never get beyond their understanding of the game. I have seen many other teachers' students leave the game because they couldn't "break through" or win under pressure. The students concluded that because they didn't win, their practice was useless. They were frustrated, feeling that their performance wasn't indicative of their practice.

This is the limit of Western Practice, Western Mind. This is why the gross scores of amateurs have not gone down despite technological leaps that have crippled many golf courses under professionals' play. Amateur golfers must accept the limitations of Western Practice.

Practice brings technical mastery under a given set of conditions. When the mind and spirit are placed in a different setting, particularly competition, technical mastery is not sufficient. Almost all competitive golfers have the same technical mastery. If you want a particular outcome, you will put pressure on yourself. And that pressure will invade the consciousness. Your desire will influence the execution of your shots, yet you will often produce the undesireable. The tighter you cling to something, the faster it will run through your fingers. Eastern Performance doesn't cling. It flows.

If you were to study the notion of Zen on the other half of the globe, you would do so though the practice one of the traditional arts: archery, swordsmanship, flower arranging, and/or tai chi. In the case of archery and swordsmanship, the art is both practical and metaphysical. It is easy to see how either could have been at one time a matter of life or death, and yet Easterners have always viewed these more as opportunities for the advancement of consciousness than self-defense. There are many things we can learn from the way in which masters of these arts teach, and as much from the way in which their pupils practice.

First, the Eastern practice is purposeless, aimless. The goal of practice initially is to develop some rudimentary technique that can be built upon. In archery, a target is merely an afterthought. Hitting a bull's-eye would be considered lucky, and would really offer no insight into your future progress. In fact, it is often said that people who have great success early will be the hardest to fall upon the rocks later in their progress. This sounds remarkably similar to golf, doesn't it?

Purposeless practice starts by becoming aware of what is going on inside, rather than what is occurring on the outside. It is more important, initially, for a teacher to know your thought process, your inner dialogue, than to watch your swing plane or ball-flight. This is because the goal is not to hit a target, but to become purposeless, selfless, aim-less, and to allow the shot to happen. Put differently, you cannot truly experience a perfect shot unless you are allowed to step aside and both perform and watch it. This is a tremendously difficult concept to grasp.

Think of your most insightful moments. What were you doing? For me, I find that inspiration strikes in the dark, or when my mind is most calm. Many writers that I know tell me that they are most inspired just before they fall asleep, or when they are driving a car. Isn't it strange that they per-form at their peak when they are distracted in apparently brainless activities? If you ask any professional golfer, this is exactly the state from which he performs his best. Learning to master this state of mind requires that you approach the game from an Eastern perspective.

Practicing with purposelessness allows you to become more aware of the internal dialogue that would typically be obscured by a wandering mind.

To integrate this skill, practice with purpose, with a focused trajectory. Review your Practice Plan and Maintain Present Moment Awareness. On the course, try to remain purpose-less and process-focused, remembering that the key to bal-ance in practice and play is Western Practice, Eastern Performance.

BE, DO, HAVE

"Desire, ask, believe, receive."
-Stella Terrill Mann

Another way of redirecting your thoughts toward performance is to think of the above phrase: be, do, have. Most people believe that improving performance is about improving what you do. If you change what you do, you will have different results, and be transformed by the outcomes. You will suddenly BE a professional golfer, a scratch player. I would like to suggest a different approach.

If you make the decision to be a better golfer, you will do different things on the golf course and practice range, and you will ultimately have lower scores. And trust me, this is not a matter of semantics or splitting hairs.

I am proposing that most people approach the game 180-degrees differently. Imagine for a minute you had Phil Mickelson's approach to the game, or Tiger Wood's. You would see the course differently, you would practice differently, you would allocate your time and mental energy differently, and you would perform differently. I suspect that Mickelson or Woods could take your swing, unchanged, exactly as it is, and shoot par or better with it because they can think their way around a golf course, can manage their game and emotions, and have learned not to struggle unnecessarily on the course. They have made the cognitive commitment that they are world-class players and wouldn't allow a missed putt, missed fairway, or swing collapse deter them from demonstrating their mastery on the next shot. More importantly, they would never waste energy by being upset or disappointed on the course. They have made a commitment to being what they are. The doing and having follow.

I have a pupil who is as talented as any player in the world. He is one of the highest rated and most consistently performing PGA Professionals in the country, and yet he is not on the PGA Tour. When I asked him what was holding him back, he said, "money." He has spent the better part of his 20s working as an assistant PGA professional, managing golf operations and pro shops, teaching, and playing in local and sectional events. He has been living from paycheck to paycheck more worried about rent than the stage on which his game should be played.

My student made the cognitive commitment many years ago that money would decide his future, rather than his talent or the number of people willing to support him. Money was the deciding factor, and because he was not wealthy, because backers have only now rushed to support him, he lost an opportunity to play on the world stage. He was trapped in the habit of do, have, be. He felt that if he performs well, he will have money, and he will be on the PGA Tour. This is a reasonable approach, but not always optimal. Not optimal because he is waiting on others to decide his future. He will consider himself a great player only when others see him as such. And, let me assure you, he has been a great player for many years already. Some would say he didn't have the self-confidence.

This is really only another way of saying he was doing instead of being. If he had decided years ago that he was a great player, if he began being that player and allowing what he did and have to follow, the outcome would have been different. He has learned invaluable lessons through his experiences, lessons that I hope will shape and fortify his game in the future. In the future, however, he will decide to be before doing. Our lives are too short to spend excess energy wondering whether we belong or whether we are worthy or complete. If we simply decided that we were enough, were lovable, were competent, were successful, and behaved in accordance with that cognitive commitment, our outcomes would be consistently and predictably different.

BECOMING PROCESS FOCUSED

"The good life is a process, not a state of being. It is a direction not a destination."
-Carl Rogers

Optimal performance requires planting the correct positive thought into your subconsciousness at the moment prior to execution. If your mind is racing, fumbling through past misses, worrying about the line or the lie, or focused upon the score rather than executing the shot at hand, you run the risk of planting a "bad seed" prior to the moment of execution. Becoming present focused through an awareness of your breathing slows down the thought process, giving you greater control and predictability over the thoughts you will drop into your subconscious prior to the moment of execution.

DRILL:

1. Focus on your breathing. Notice the pace, depth, and quality of the breath passing in and out of your lungs. Is your breathing becoming faster or slower as you notice its rhythm?

2. Take a long deep inhalation through both nostrils, holding the breath with the deepest portion of your diaphragm for less than a second before very slowly and evenly allowing the breath to escape through your mouth. Repeat this

three times, again filling your lungs to 100% capacity. Notice any sensations in your body. Are you agitated or nervous, frightened or incredulous? Repeat the exercise as necessary to achieve a state of listlessness or deep calm awareness. This is the state from which your best golf will blossom.

3. Think of an intimidating Par 3 with a long carry over water or a downhill five foot right-breaking putt on 18 to shoot 79. Notice any tension in your chest, forearms, back, or neck. With that tension, are you likely to carry the water or hit the putt firm and center-cut? Now try the breathing exercise above.

4.   Once you've completed the breathing exercise, try visualizing the shot again. Notice how easy it is to see your-self making the putt, carrying the ball high over the water and landing softly near the pin.

"The present is the future of our past."
-Karl Popper

"Now or never! You must live in the present, launch yourself on every wave, find your eternity in each moment."
-Henry David Thoreau

BREATHWORK

In practice, I often see young pros listening to headphones, relaxing, and working on their breathing. Tennis pros Gabriela Sabatini and Pete Sampras, as well as NBA Hall of Famer Patrick Ewing regularly listened to music and practiced breathing techniques prior to a match or game. NBA Hall of Famer Scottie Pippin paused and took two breaths before each free throw. Greg Louganis would regularly wait what seemed like minutes on the diving board until he felt that he had taken a fully relaxed breath before executing a dive.

Psychologist Dorothy Harris developed the following exercise that can assist athletes to focus and center themselves during practice and competition.

Step One. Imagine that your lungs are divided into three separate parts: a lower, middle, and upper section. Think of each of these sections having a color: green, yellow, and red. Close your eyes and imagine that you are filling just the bottom, or green, third of your lungs as you inhale. Imagine as you do so stretching your diaphragm to full extension and hold the breath just a moment before allowing a slow controlled exhale.

Step Two. Now imagine filling the second third, or yellow

section, of your lungs. Feel your chest and ribcage expand as you fill your lungs to full capacity. Hold the stretch just a moment before allowing a slow controlled exhale.

Step Three. Finally, fill the last section, the red portion, raising your chest and shoulders as you do so. Feel as though you are being lifted off of your feet as you do so. Hold the breath for a moment and slowly release on the exhale.

Complete all of the stages with soft, smooth breaths. Set the intention to breathe in positive fulfilling energy and to exhale any limitation or negativity. Set up environmental cues to remind you to begin the breathing exercise, such as the moment you pull a club or as you pace yardage or measure a putt.

ASSIGNMENT:

Try this drill for at least five minutes in your car (parked) before heading to the bag drop or driving range. Listen to soothing music and practice breathing into the three zones. Resolve to have mastered your breathwork before setting foot on the course

EVALUATING ON-COURSE PERFORMANCE

This chart is extremely useful if you are having difficulty scoring. If you want to lower your scoring average, ball striking and driving distance are not important statistics. Consistent scoring requires solid performance in five areas: Fairways Hit, Greens in Regulation, Putts, Up & Downs, and Present Moment Awareness. Improvement in one area will tend to lead to improvement in others. For instance, hitting fairways makes hitting greens easier; hitting greens leads to more birdie opportunities, and getting close to greens leads to easier up and downs. I've added maintaining present moment awareness because scoring is not something you can improve solely by thinking. You can't think ahead on a hole, deciding to hit a fairway or deciding to hit a green. You can only control the moment to moment awareness of your surroundings. When players absorb themselves in the moment, completely devote themselves to the shot at hand, scores improve. When players become score or mechanics focused, scoring suffers. The following are some guidelines to improving performance in the five key areas.

HOLE:	1	2	3	4	5	6	7	8	9	10	11	12	13	14	15	16	17	18	TOTALS
FAIRWAYS HIT	✓		✓	✓		✓	✓		✓	✓		✓		✓					9 of 14
GREENS HIT	✓		✓			✓		✓	✓			✓							6 of 18
UP & DOWNS		✓		X	X	✓		X		X		X	✓		✓	X	X	X	4 of 12
PUTTS	2	2	2	2	2	2	3	1	3	2	2	2	2	2	2	1	2	2	36
PRESENT MOMENT AWARENESS	A	C	C	C	A	C	B	B	D	B	B	B	B	C	B	A	B	B	B-

HOLE:	1	2	3	4	5	6	7	8	9	10	11	12	13	14	15	16	17	18	TOTALS
FAIRWAYS HIT																			
GREENS HIT																			
UP & DOWNS																			
PUTTS																			
PRESENT MOMENT AWARENESS																			

Fairways Hit: Shooting par requires being in the fairway. The straighter you hit the ball, the shorter the hole becomes, and lies are almost always better from the short grass. Being in the fairway also reduces the number of barriers you must hit around, and courses are usually designed with collars or landing areas that can be employed if you're hitting from the fairway. If you want to break par, plan on hitting at least 10 of the 14 fairways on the Par 4s and Par 5s most courses provide.

Greens Hit in Regulation: Getting on greens quickly is an obvious way to improve scoring. Inconsistent ball strikers can make up for poor performance by always aiming to the safe or center portion of the green, avoiding hitting over or around trouble, and on Par 5s playing conservatively to ensure being on the putting surface on their third shot. Modern technology makes going for Par 5s in two possible, but not necessarily probable. Getting on the green in three every time will beat hitting on in two once or twice a year. Final note: among amateur players, Par 3s are the vortex of scoring. Par 3s should rarely be approached as birdie holes. Your goal is to get the ball on the middle or safe portion of the green and two-putt. Remember to be extremely precise with your target off the tee. Most players either hit to too large a target or go pin seeking. Play to a tiny spot on the green. If you two-putt, you've done your job. If you happen to sink a long putt, it's a bonus. Making pars on a course's Par 3s is a quick way to make shooting par a realistic long-term goal.

Putts: Reducing the number of putts in a round is the easiest way to improve scoring. Great putters are great scorers. Working to see the ball in the hole and becoming focused only upon speed is the fastest way to improve your putting. Don't worry about how far the ball will run away, the roll, or the condition of the green. If you focus only on speed after you've set down your putter, you'll be amazed at how many putts will drop. Also, be completely committed to your putts. If your head is snapping up to look at where your ball is going, you're not committed to the stroke, line, or speed. Don't take the putter back until you know exactly how hard you're going to hit the putt on the line you've chosen. If you do these things correctly, you're likely to see at least a two putt per round improvement.

Up & Downs: Tiger Woods has consistently credited his success to scrambling. While professionals are happy to get the ball up and down 50-60% of the time, Woods finds a way to get the ball up and in about 75-80% of his opportunities. Working on the short game is mostly about practice and touch. Once you have a consistent routine, solid take-away, and descending impact, the rest is imagination and present moment awareness. Spend all of your energy imag-ining the ball going in the hole. Don't think mechanics, just execute. And never think about up and downs. Think up and ins. Trying to make every shot inside 100 yards will make all the difference in your scoring.

Present Moment Awareness: Improved present moment awareness guarantees improved scoring. Players who stand over shots and think about possible disasters or glory aren't allowing their brains to focus on the important things in a swing: rhythm, breathing, and target. Become completely aware of the shot at hand and eliminate the wandering thoughts that lead to disaster. Being completely present moment aware will change your golfing experience. Four hour rounds will seem half as long, and when you go back to add your scores, don't be surprised if you're well under your stroke average. Players who add their scores on the course are building pressure. Pressure leads to tension and tension leads to errors. Being present moment aware elim-inates pressure and tension, and frees the body to execute the shots you see in your mind's eye.

Whether you're trying to break 100 or stay consistently in the 70s, as long as you have room for improvement in these five areas, you have the ability to go lower.

"People become what they think about
themselves"

Mohandas Karamchand Gandhi

HOW TO PRACTICE

"Practice, which some regard as a chore, should be approached as just about the most pleasant recreation ever devised."

-Babe Didrikson

There are really very few keys to successful practice. The most important is to spend at least 50% of the total time you devote to practice and play to the short game. This includes chipping, pitching, bunker play, shots inside 100 yards, and putting. Many players play once a week, practice an hour or two, and think that spending 15-20 minutes on the putting green is enough to improve their game. This is not a successful strategy. I encourage players to spend at least 2 hours a week putting, and at least 2 more on chipping, pitching, and shots inside 100 yards. The best players in the world will tell you that unless you can get the ball inside 10 feet from within 100 yards and make the putt 70% of the time, you have not mastered the critical part of the game.

When practicing your full swing, remember to stretch and warm up for at least five minutes. This is a difficult habit to teach, but it will improve performance. A student of mine would regularly start hot and cool off quickly on the course. In time, we learned that he never stretched his muscles properly, and by the time he was making the turn, his body was fatigued from the stress he had placed on his muscles. Walking for at least five minutes and five minutes of stretching will give you sustained energy on the course and a more repeatable swing.

When practicing your full swing start with any club in their bag, as long as it has a 7 on the bottom. Spend the most time with your mid-irons, wedges, and driver. These should become your money clubs. If you're hitting a lot of long-irons, your driving is the problem. No one ever gained confidence relying on his long-irons to save his game. The game is about driving accurately, safe approach shots, and a good short game. Take that thought as you approach your full swing.

DRILL:

Try this warm-up before playing:

Take a short five minute walk and stretch your hamstrings, lower back, shoulders, and arms for five minutes. Get comfortable with your mid-irons. Hit 20 balls with a smooth fluid swing. Move to your pitching and sand wedge, hitting 15 shots each. Hit 20 balls with the driver, working from 70% of your power up to 90%. Hit 5 shots with a 3-wood, 2 or 3 long irons, then finish with four well-targeted wedges and four well-targeted drives. As you hit those last drives, envision the shot you will hit off the first tee. Are you going to hit it high or low, and with what ball shape? See all the variables and execute at least three successful shots before walking comfortably to the First Tee.

HUMILITY

"In theory there is no difference between theory and practice. In practice there is."
-Yogi Berra

"Too much humility is pride."
-German Proverb

The reason most people languish in mediocrity is that they fail to take risks at appropriate times. More often than not, fear grips a golfer at critical moments, causing balls to sail out of bounds, into the water, or far short of the hole on an already short putt. Fear is golf's greatest killer, and its power lingers off the course as well. We fail to challenge ourselves, we fail to acknowledge where we must improve, and ironically, I believe, because of a lack of humility. We believe we must perform at a certain level in order to feel good about ourselves. If we don't shoot, 75, 85, 95, we are defeated, deflated, and spent. The story of the golfer throwing his clubs into the water only to jump in after them moments later reminds us that we all are humbled by the game. Withdrawal is not the answer.

In order to be a good golfer, you must believe in your ability and that the ball will go where you intend it to go. Without this belief, you are assured failure. You must believe in your ability, yet have the humility to accept when things don't go as planned. People fall into patterns of missed shots because they failed to accept the first bad shot they hit. Even great players miss shots. They hit it out of bounds. They miss two-footers. The difference between a

great player and a poor one is that great players accept the
inevitability of hitting bad shots, and are immediately sure
that they won't happen again. Some players "blame away"
their missed shots, saying that the error was because of a
bad lie, bad advice from a caddie, or caused by a flaw in the
green. Great players know that those hiccups are part of the
game and accept them in an impersonal and humble man-
ner.

The next time you feel yourself lapsing into a train of negative thoughts, ask yourself "What's the Worst That Could
Happen?" or "What If?" What's the worst that will happen
if you miss a putt or hit it out of bounds? What's the worst
that will happen if you snap a club, lose a tournament, or
whiff on the first tee? Maybe people would laugh? Maybe
your pride would be hurt? Everyone I know sustained some
ridicule a teenager. You survived, and you'll survive whatever happens to you on the golf course. Remember that.
The better players become the less they are able to master
this skill. A shot is just a shot. It is not an indicator of
future success, and it is not a representation of your work.
Approach each shot with humility and leave each shot with
as much. Remember that slumps are a product of a chain
of negative thoughts, usually tied to perfectionism and a
lack of acceptance. When you find yourself exhibiting
either of these characteristics, ask yourself "What If?" and
remember that no matter how many times you ask that
question, the worst that can happen is rarely life-threaten-
ing. Take chances; enjoy the difficulty of the game, and
humbly accept whatever happens.

THE SHORT GAME

"You drive for show, but putt for dough"
-Bobby Locke

Golf can be divided into four different events: driving, approach shots, putting, and the short game. People tend to see the game in that order of importance, feeling that driving is the most critical, followed by approach shots, followed by putting, and coming in a very distant last is chipping and pitching. In reality, the game is about getting the ball in the hole, and it doesn't take Albert Einstein to figure out that putting is the most important, followed by, perhaps surprisingly, the short game.

If you read Tiger Woods' How I Play Golf, there is an astounding acknowledgement in his discussion of his scrambling statistics. Tiger doesn't need to hit as many greens or fairways because he will get the ball up or in almost 85% of the time, astounding considering that most other touring professionals would be satisfied with doing so 65% of the time. The short game requires excellent technique, but also a solid mental approach.

See the ball going into the hole: This is the critical element. Many players who wind up short with chips and pitches could solve their problems simply by practicing seeing the ball going into the hole. Every great player in the world should expect the ball to go in the hole. I guarantee that Ernie Els, who consistently chips in at least once a round, isn't thinking, "Just get it inside 6 feet."

DRILLS:

Scoring: During your next round of golf, play from the middle of the fairway.

> Place a ball 100-yards from the green on all par 5s and keep your score as if you were lying two.

> Place a ball 150 yards from the green on all par 4s and keep your score as if you were lying 1.

> On Par 3s, place a ball on the middle of the green, keeping your score as if you were lying 1.

Most people believe that breaking par would be easy from these positions. Not true. While it is statistically much more probable that you will approach par from these positions, most amateurs will score NO BETTER than their regular 18-hole score (minus penalty strokes). Don't believe me? Try the drill.

Draw Back: Putt to a hole more than 20 feet away. If you miss the first putt, draw the ball back the length of your putter, approximately 3feet. Try to make the lengthened comebacker. This drill assists you with speed control as well as making "critical length" putts inside four feet.

Double Draw Back: This is essentially the same drill as Draw Back, except that you draw the ball back two putter lengths, approximately six feet, after the initial putt and try to make the much lengthened comebacker.

Hole Out: Measure your progress by makes, not misses.

Surround a Hole: Scatter between 10 and 20 balls three feet around a hole. Work your way around the circle, making each putt. If you miss a putt, replace the balls and begin again. Don't leave the practice green until you can make the putts from all sides of a hole. This drill is especially useful if you putt to a hole with break. It forces you to learn the difference in speeds and alignment required to hit left-to-right and right-to-left putts (hint: they're not the same).

Never Take a Putt You're Not Going to Make: Missing putts breed indecision and uncertainty, both of which create tentative or overly aggressive putting strokes. In practice, train your brain to make every putt by putting to the hole only when inside five feet. For most players, this is a difficult transition to make in practice, but if you begin to putt to the hole only from one foot, and slowly work your way out on subsequent practice sessions, you will master the short putts quickly, and have greater confidence on the green no matter how long the putt.

Putt to a Tee: Keeping in mind that you should never putt to a hole unless you can guarantee you'll make the putt, on putts longer than five feet, putt to a tee. This assists you with focusing on the smallest of possible targets, and to remind you that you must get the ball past the target.

Putt to the Far Fringe: This drill is similar to lagging in billiards, and is the first putting drill I use in my pre-game warm-up. Using one ball, putt from any spot on the green to the edge of the fringe at least 20 feet away. Putt across the green, from fringe to fringe, until you have mastered the speed and general contouring of the green. If you practice this drill before every round, you'll never have problem reading the speed of greens again.

From the Fringe: Start with three balls on the fringe of a practice green. Using your preferred chipping club, chip all of the balls toward a specific hole (remember to try to make each shot). For the balls you don't chip in, try to make the putts with the club you chipped with. Your goal is to take no more than five strokes (three chips and hopefully only two putts). Repeat the drill using a variety of clubs. This drill will reinforce the importance of speed and alignment on chipping.

From Way Downtown: Set out three trash cans or laundry baskets 15, 20, and 30 yards out and start "making baskets" with your sand and lob wedges.

Wind the Clock: Imagining that your left arm is the minute hand on a clock, hit pitches, progressively farther from one another, imagining that you are swinging the club from 7:00 to 6:00, 7:30 to 6:00, 8:00 to 6:00 and so on. Once you have reached 9:30, begin to work your way back, dropping balls inside the ones you previously hit.

Putt to the Apex: On a putt that breaks at least six inches in one direction, place a tee at the apex of the break. Learn to putt toward that tee or apex with a smooth confident stroke.

This reduces being tentative or overly aggressive, imparting improper spin on the ball. Remember, "Every putt is a straight putt" (Bobby Locke).

Make a Ball Stop: Work on controlling how far a ball will roll or skip after it lands by adjusting the face of the club. Don't try to spin the ball or help it in any way. Work on contact and trajectory. Spin is a byproduct of these two variables.

Three Balls Inside 100: Begin working on your distance control on the "money shots" (those between 20 and 60 yards) by tossing three balls at distances between 20 and 60 yards using an underhanded motion and trying to make all three. Remember to see the ball going in the hole. Using your eyes is critical. Feel follows your ability to visualize the ball going in. After you're comfortable tossing balls at the hole, practice pitch shots with your wedges, taking the same amount of backswing you used when tossing under-handed.

The String: Tie a pencil at each end of a five foot long piece of string. Put one pencil into the green on the far side of the cup and place the other pencil in the ground on the near side, stretching the string tightly, so that it hovers over the ground like a tightrope. Practice putting with the club face remaining square under the string for the entire stroke. Repeat the drill until you can consistently make 10 putts in a row. Use increasing lengths of string to build confidence on longer putts.

Aladdin's Carpet: Draw a rectangular box in the sand trap about six inches long toward the target and four inches across. Place a ball in the middle of the box. When Aladdin rode on his carpet, the entire carpet rose at once. Bunker play is no different. Think of making the carpet fly to the green in one piece. If the carpet goes to the target, Aladdin will go to the target. Forget the ball. Focus on the carpet.

Competitions

Hoot Scoot: Scatter a bucket of balls around a green and take turns with a partner, seeing how many balls you both can get up and in within two strokes. Alternate choosing the ball and playing in, but keep a running total of who makes more and who gets up and down more often.

Side by Side: With your partner, stand at different holes and putt toward the hole closest to your partner. Try to make putts of at least 20 feet. If one of you makes a putt, switch sides. Repeat the drill until one partner makes 10 or 20.

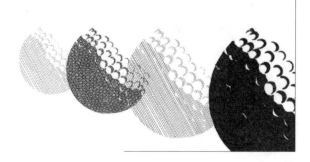

> "You must be the change you wish to see
> in the world."

Mohandas Karamchand Gandhi

TYPE SPECIFIC
EXCERCISES

Knowing the strengths and limitations of your Type allows you to focus your energy toward particular trajectories. The following section offers Type-specific exercises designed to take advantage of the personality-performance relationship.

CRUSADER

"Consider how much more you often suffer from your anger and grief, than from those very things for which you are angry and grieved."
-Marcus Antonius

In the book, Golf in the Kingdom, the mystical figure Shivas Irons holes out from the tee on a long Par 3 over a crevasse in the pitch of night. Before he swings, he unleashes a terrible cry, a howl that frightens the main character, Michael Murphy. In order to perform at their highest, Crusaders must release their anger, must decide in advance to release their tension, and do so by pouring their selves and their souls into the shot. In spiritual terms, the Crusader must practice Kenosis, or the emptying of the soul in order to fulfill his possibilities. The following are some exercises designed to assist you in pouring yourself into the game.

1. Growl, howl, or spit before every swing. Work it into your routine. Acknowledge your anger and frustration and use it to your advantage. If you plan to play angry, it's impossible for your anger to sneak up on you.

2. Give in to your passion. Crusaders often make the mistake of displacing their passion into petty jealousies or regrets. More than any other type, the Crusader must commit to a Vision Statement that draws from his deep conviction and love for the game. Crusaders are the easiest to get knocked off track when things go wrong on the course, so be constantly familiar with the following phrase: "Is this emo-

tion taking me closer or farther away from my goal?" With this question always on the front of the mind, a Crusader's passion can easily be honed into improved performance.

3. As an aid to his mental game, Ben Hogan would hold onto his club after a shot and release it only after he reached the next shot in order to keep himself mentally in the game. Try the drill with a golf club, or make a habit using physical objects, such as touching a bag tag before drawing a club and starting your preshot routine. Basketball players will sometimes touch their face or arms before a free throw to start a chain reaction of positive mental practices. Use one of these techniques to center yourself before and between shots.

ADVISOR

"Pride goeth before destruction, and a haughty spirit before a fall."

-Proverbs (Chapter 16, Verse 18)

The best teachers can make the best or worst students. Advisors regularly come to the course with a game plan and razor-like ability to decide what to do under pressure. They appear to be excellent surveyors of the territory, and yet this is the key to the Advisor's failure. Advisors must relinquish their "knowing" in order to excel. They must learn to open their minds to new possibilities, even miracles. Instead of being trapped into a particular way of thinking that has already demonstrated a historical track record, Advisors must learn to "think outside the box," "be spontaneous," and "go with the flow." It is ultimately a willingness to surrender and be humble that will lead to an Advisor's greatest triumphs.

1. Play alone. Advisors' greatest gains can be made when left to solitary exploration. When an Advisor is left alone on the course, he may feel uncomfortable or find his mind wandering. Keep track of the thoughts and remind yourself why you play the game.

2. Get selfish. Of all the Types, Advisors are the last to spend money on nice clubs, clothes, or weekend rounds. They are also the least likely to give up the expectations of those around them. If you're not already playing regularly because of the obligations you've made, it's time to recon-

sider your priorities. Self care includes taking the time to explore your passions. Practically, an ounce of prevention is worth a pound of cure. Taking care of yourself now will support your efforts and others down the line.

3. Make a list of simple pleasures, particularly those having to do with golf. Force yourself to indulge yourself once a day. Remember that you must devote at least 10% of your energy to improve. If you're already spending 10%, spend 20%. Ultimately, it is the Advisor's willingness to give into their selfish love of the game that leads to enhanced performance.

ACHIEVER

All is not what it seems. An Achiever is the quickest to succeed, and yet the most likely to have hollow joy and unfulfilling glory. The Achiever must grapple with his own sadness and indecisiveness, his own wonder over his course in life. He must face whatever is happening on the course as an expression of the limitations of his life, take a deep breath, and accept the limitations as part of the universal order. Limitations can be allies and direction markers telling us to go another way, but Achievers often barrel through the warning signs, assuring themselves and others that rules and records were meant to be broken. The following are exercises to maximize Achievers' strengths and to assist with minimizing their weaknesses.

1. List your fears. Spend at least an hour writing down the things you fear and avoid. Be as specific and graphic as possible. When you have exhausted your fears, spend a moment reflecting on the amount of energy you spend worrying about or trying to prevent these outcomes.

2. Imagine yourself without fear. Spend at least fifteen minutes writing down what you'd do without your fears. Again, be as graphic and detailed as possible.

MYSTIC

> "Envy is the daughter of pride, the author of murder and revenge, the beginner of secret sedition and the perpetual tormentor of virtue. Envy is the filthy slime of the soul; a venom, a poison, or quicksilver which consumeth the flesh and drieth up the marrow of the bones."
>
> -Socrates

Nothing is missing from your life. Nothing is missing from your game. Spending time to refine the gifts that you have will serve the you best. Focusing on the positives and committing yourself to a plan of action are the sure ways to enhanced performance. Retooling swings, changing clubs, and endless tinkering are common Mystic mistakes. Indecisiveness and self-doubt often follow a Mystic's envy. Try the following drills to maximize the Mystic's better qualities.

1. Refuse to be discouraged. Of all the Types, Mystics are the most likely to fall into despair over their performance or lack of improvement. Mystics need to be constantly reassured that they are headed in the right direction, but also need their own assistance in remaining positive. Make a weekly list of the areas in which you've improved. Commit ahead of time that if you're not improved in any area, you'll only dwell on where you can improve most quickly, and commit to a practice plan that can get you back on track.

2. Develop a solid practice plan. In the back of the book you'll find a sample practice plan, outlining how some play-

ers approach improving their performance. Mystics MUST develop and use a thorough practice plan. If possible, give the plan to a colleague or playing partner who can gently support you by reminding you to stick to the routine you've established. Devote yourself to a practice plan for at least three months and don't allow yourself to change mid-term. Consistent devotion to basic principles is the Mystic's key for improved performance.

THINKER

Because golf is a mental game, Thinkers are predisposed to performing well. They often perform better in private, where they can hone the skills they intuitively know they must improve. They can be secretive about their game, and sneaky about their progress and improvement. The key to the Thinker's mastery of the game is that he must fight. Thinkers must develop an ability to get in an opponent's face, to put their foot on a competitor's throat when he's down. Passion needs to be put into the quest for competitive and cooperative excellence.

1. Partner Up. Thinkers require a compatriot they can play with and compete against. When Thinkers play by themselves or with other Thinkers, the game is often enlightening, but rarely intense and passionate. Ideally, a Thinker would pair up with a Joker, someone boisterous and obnoxious, someone that pushes all of a Thinker's buttons. Thinkers must overcome their distaste for getting their hands dirty, and begin to engage and enjoy the prospect of taking risks, winning ugly, and the bitterness of close defeats.

2. Win Ugly and Love It. Thinkers often have a slow building negative emotional reaction to their shots not

being perfect. Unlike Achievers, Thinkers won't typically overreact or throw tantrums, but they can slowly go away in a round or tournament, barely being aware of themselves or surroundings by the 18th Hole. Winning Ugly is the solution. Thinkers have to develop a sneakiness about bad shots, and this is another time where an excellent short game can destroy an opponent or save a round. Thinkers must have great escape shots and develop an affinity for getting the ball in the hole, rather than a flawlessly executed game plan.

3.   The Mystic Wing. One of the Thinker's wings (or neighbor) on the Enneagram is The Mystic. Thinkers can tend toward this Type, explaining their subtle talents of creativity and sensitivity. Use these tendencies around the greens. With the ability to be magical from bunkers, the fringe, and inside 100 yards, the Thinker can be a dominant player.

SKEPTIC

The Skeptic's obedience to safe, responsible practice and play is a recipe for disaster. Obeying the rules will not lead to long or short-term success, nor will manic overdoing or rushing. As a players and people, Skeptics must learn to stretch their comfort zones, one day at a time. Rome was not built in a day, and despite the Skeptic's intense wishes, progress will come slowly, perhaps paradoxically, by greater and greater discomforts. Try the following to develop an ability to stretch gradually, to trade caution for systematic aggressiveness.

1. Start hitting driver. Begin to spend most of your full-swing practice hitting the driver, and hit driver on every Par 4 or Par 5 you play, regardless of the danger.

2. To develop a more aggressive swing, practice hitting your driver to different distances. Begin by hitting it only 50 yards. Hit the next shot 60. Hit the third shot 70 yards, and continue until you are pushing past whatever your longest drive is. If you find yourself overswinging, work your way back toward 50 yards until you have found the proper rhythm and tempo. But immediately reverse and work toward your maximum drive. Don't take your most aggressive swing to the course, but plan on hitting it 90% all

day long.

3. Putt to the back of the hole. Skeptics overread putts and almost always leave them on the short side of the hole. Take the break out of the putts and begin to hit them at the back of the hole. See the ball traveling over the front edge with enough roll to get it past the hole. If in doubt about the line of a putt, hit it hard and at the middle. Trust that you'll make the comebacker.

4. Trust a coach. Find a coach with whom you can relate, and commit to seeing that person for at least a year. This is a challenge for most Skeptics, but consistency is important. Accept the challenges a coach offers and accept responsibility if things go awry. For this reason, you'll need to do some research into the most suitable instructors. Make your decision about your coach by researching thoroughly. You'll be glad you did.

JOKER

"Gluttony is not a secret vice."
-Orson Welles

The Joker's lust for the game can be contagious, but also compulsive. Jokers walk the fine line between aggressiveness and destruction and can fall short of their goals not because of lack of talent or practice but out of impulsivity and impatience. The spontaneity of the Joker is the fuel for a great player, but acceptance and patience are the virtues that this Type must master in order to excel.

1. Make Decisions Ahead of Time. Course management begins before you get to the course. More than any other Type, Jokers must develop a solid game plan, and practice executing the shots in the mind prior to stepping onto the first tee. More than any other Type, Jokers will want to stray from the game plan. Be consistent. Make decisions ahead of time, not under pressure.

2. Be a Neutral Observer. As often as possible, see yourself as someone whom you don't know might see you. Put yourself in the other person's shoes and think about what kind of decisions he might suggest to you. Making decisions from a calm but empathetic position will lead to better choices.

3. When in Doubt, Choose the Safest Path. If you come to a decision you haven't accounted for, play safe. Keep the ball in the fairway, play to the middle of greens. You can be

aggressive inside 100 yards, but the rest of the time, always choose the safe path. Even if it feels or looks as though safe didn't work out, it will reward you in the end.

MAVERICK

"...power can mean one of two things, domination or potency. Far from being identical, these two qualities are mutually exclusive. Impotence, using the term not only with regard to the sexual sphere but to all spheres of human potentialities, results in the sadistic striving for domination; to the extent to which an individual is potent, that is, able to realize his potentialities on the basis of freedom and integrity of his self, he does not need to dominate and is lacking the lust for power. Power, in the sense of domination, is the perversion of potency, just as sexual sadism is the perversion of sexual love."

- Erich Fromm

Mavericks possess an intensely passion that can inspire others to great feats. In order for the Maverick to soar, however, he must develop an unconscious ability to stay in the moment, avoid unnecessary highs and lows, and control the sometimes explosiveness of his passion. Like Jokers, Mavericks excel under pressure, love the hardest of shots, the most difficult of challenges. However, this predisposes them to streaky play and foolish decisions. Mavericks must learn to love the expression of the plans that they have developed, to acquire an appreciation for the routines of practice and the difficulty of maintaining focus and precision over a four-hour round. But most importantly, the Maverick must hold his cards close to the vest. He must trade his leadership for quiet strength and gentle self-forgiveness and praise. The following exercises are designed to maximize a Maverick's performance.

1. Take 20 steps. Early in his career, Tiger Woods was notorious for slamming clubs into the ground during fits of rage that disrupted the flow of his round. He carried missed shots down the fairway, allowing the negativity to multiply. To combat this pattern, he allowed himself 20 steps to be as upset as he wanted, but by the 20th step, he committed to be completely focused on the next. You might say that every step was lightening the pressure until he was mentally light as a feather before he stepped to the ball and began the preshot routine for the next shot. Studies on professional and Olympic athletes tell us that tantruming is more likely to lead to success than total suppression of emotions, but that the optimal strategy is to cycle through the highs and the lows quickly. Don't allow the peaks to get too high, or the valleys grow too low. Be happy and sad, angry and elated, but do it in 20 steps.

2. Wear a Mask. Like David Duval, I used to wear protective eyewear to keep sand and debris out of my eyes during play. After a series of matches, I realized that my opponents didn't get under my skin anymore. The wrap-around glasses hid my eyes from my opponents, who were then less capable of reading and manipulate my emotions. I find that great Mavericks need assistance withdrawing from the stimuli around them. They can be overly reactive, and hiding under the brim of a wide hat or protective eyewear can limit the stimuli that they let in and out. I don't believe in controlling facial features or expressions. The emotions and physical sensations are teaching you lessons, but I don't believe in broadcasting those lessons to competitors. Express your emotions, but do so out of the view of competitors, and use your apparel to assist you in keeping your cards close to the vest.

PEACEMAKER

"Idleness is emptiness; the tree in which the sap is stagnant, remains fruitless"

-Hosea Ballou

Practice, practice, practice. The key to overcoming the Peacemaker's tendency toward complacency is to make practice and enjoyable daily activity. Working toward clear goals and trajectories can remove the fear of failure or catastrophe, a danger as Peacemakers often see many sides or possibilities to a set of circumstances. Remember that the Peacemaker is prone to simply going with the flow, rather than establishing firm boundaries or swimming upstream. Developing an inner passion and consistently displaying it on the course will make Peacemakers excellent players.

1. Commit to Doing One Practice-Related Activity Per Day. Unlike many of the other types, Peacemakers don't have to reach for monumental change in order to improve. Simply doing one thing a day, periodically changing the routine to keep the practice interesting, will lead to success. You might commit to working on six footers for an hour then switch to driving for an hour the next day. What you do isn't as important as that you do something. Developing a love for practice requires keeping it fresh and flexible. Until you have a finely tuned love for practice, working on your deficits will not be fruitful. A firmly established practice routine will enhance your enjoyment of practice and play.

2. Explore Your Resistance at Home. Peacemakers are a

difficult Type to coach because they require a tremendous amount of introspection. They are critical of their own abilities and are keenly aware of the spiritual ebb and flow of their own mastery. Peacemakers are the golfers who will leave behind half a bucket of balls at the range because things weren't going well, and it just wasn't fun. The key to overcoming frustration and self-criticism is to schedule time for self-reflection and doubt at home. I once had a Peacemaker who would all but give up in tournaments when he felt things weren't "feeling right." He was deciding whether to pursue a professional career during tournament play. When he scheduled time to journal or talk about his feelings with his wife at home, and when he agreed not to explore his resistance on the course or in practice, he found his fears and resistance stayed at home, and his enthusiasm and for the game blossomed on the course. If you have doubts about the game, explore them at home.

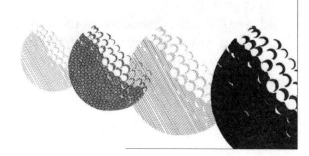

CONCLUSION

When I asked my teacher about the quality of books on sports psychology, he told me that he knew everything written in any book on the subject. He had been a member of the PGA Tour, instructed PGA Tour Players who won major championships, and was regarded among the best golf instructors in the world, so I didn't doubt his wisdom, but he said he wasn't alone in knowing what was in books. He taught that every great player has all of the skills listed in this book or any other on the subject. They may not know they have them, but they do, and they'll recognize the skills when seen in print. Even many amateur players know these skills. The problem, as my teacher taught me through years of struggle, is that they forget. Bad players forget good habits. Good players remember good habits and build them into their preshot routine, practice, and on-course performance. Great players do the things in this book, sometimes effortlessly, but often because they have practiced them for years under the pressure of their own devotion to their game.

There is no one key to improved performance. To be a great player you must identify your character, know its strengths and weaknesses, develop a plan to maximize your potential and limit your barriers, practice in a spiritual way, and learn to accept the outcomes for what they ARE, rather than what they might MEAN.

The only thing governing your progress in golf, as in life, is your willingness to accept and incorporate the lessons you have learned. There are no shortcuts. The tortoise beat the hare because his pride and lack of humility and surrender. You will achieve when you are capable of detachedly assessing your skills and developing them as they need developing. The pace is solely determined, not by diligence and rigorousness, but by patience, acceptance, and intense devotion to your vision.

Remember to be flexible, passionate, and soulful. You will succeed.

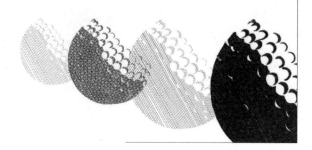

INNER GAME

Breaking Golf's Unbreakable Barriers

WORKBOOK

VISION WORKSHEET

My character Type is: _____

My Greatest Inner Strengths:

1. _____
2. _____
3. _____
4. _____
5. _____

My Values:

1. _____
2. _____
3. _____
4. _____
5. _____

My Assets:

1. _____
2. _____
3. _____
4. _____
5. _____

My Allies:

1. _____
2. _____
3. _____
4. _____
5. _____

If God would grant a miracle and I could accomplish anything, it would be to:

_____
_____
_____

At my best, I am:

_____
_____

In order to stay my best, I need to:

_____
_____

Write a vision statement that reflects your dreams and values. Write it in the present tense, remembering that the more senses you incorporate, the more passionately the words leap off the page, and the more likely they will leap into reality.

REMEMBER YOUR ASSETS

List your talents:

_____

_____

_____

_____

List all the things you love to do while expressing these unique talents:

_____

_____

_____

_____

List your allies:

_____

_____

_____

_____

List the material assets that will serve you on the course:

_____

_____

_____

_____

As you go through the various stages of enhanced performance, it's important to remember your assets. Just as a captain will inventory his cargo before setting sail, it is important that you keep a close eye on the strengths you can draw upon. You are a unique person. No other person in the universe has the exact set of talents that you possess. It is your duty and opportunity to express them. As you free your talents, you will free yourself.

ENERGY DRAINS

List the people or things that drain energy from your life:

_____

_____

_____

_____

_____

Why do you recreate your energy drains by allowing them to continue?

_____

_____

_____

_____

What would happen if you removed the energy drains?

_____

_____

What do you need to do to remove the energy drains?

_____

_____

What single step could you commit to doing for the next 30 days to assist you in removing just one of the energy drains?

_____

_____

_____

Place this in your 30-Day Action Plan and track your progress. Spend time visualizing your life without the energy drains, and you're likely to see improvement.

BARRIERS

Feelings of anxiety or guilt typically arise out of our own resistance to our deepest desires. We do what we are told to do or what others expect from us, often requiring us to ignore the things we'd rather say or do. Spend a moment thinking about a behavior that creates a barrier in your performance or enjoyment.

1. Put the problematic behavior in context. What forces act upon you when you are in this situation?

2. What are the motives and needs driving your behavior? What were you trying to satisfy or accomplish?

3. Where did you learn the behavior? Who modeled this behavior for you in your life?

4. Restate the underlying need and problem-solve as to how you could more effectively meet this need.

5. Plan a new behavior.

6. Forgive yourself and move on.

Forgiving yourself and moving on doesn't necessarily mean that you will radically alter your behaviors, but it does mean that you will radically alter the way you think about what you do and say. Remember to be gentle and patient. Growth will happen naturally.

I AM

Make a list of the positive attributes you have, or would like to have, on the golf course. Examples might be calm, confident, courageous, careful, or carefree. Make a list of these adjectives and carry them with you in your pocket until you can recite the list from memory. When you find yourself out of the zone, recite each word slowly, taking a breath before saying the word aloud, then exhaling slowly before reciting the next. This is a great way to train your mind to focus upon the positive mental attributes you'd like to carry to the next shot.

Consider the following attributes for your list:

Alive	Jovial	Sure
Aware	Jubilant	Thankful
Bold	Loose	Unwavering
Calm	Lucky	Virile
Carefree	Mischievous	Voracious
Cheerful	Nonchalant	Wise
Confident	Open	Worthy
Courageous	Overjoyed	Youthful
Dedicated	Passionate	Zealous
Energized	Peaceful	
Fearless	Powerful	
Fluid	Quiet	
Focused	Relaxed	
Gentle	Renewed	
Glorious	Reserved	
Happy	Revitalized	
Humble	Self-Assured	
Intelligent	Skilled	
Intense	Strong	

INTENTION AND DESIRES

Make a list of your desires and carry them with you. Be as specific and creative as possible, but leave open the possibility that something better for your own good or the highest good of those around you might manifest instead.

Be open to the possibility that what you seek will manifest without effort. When your intention and desires are in alignment with your purpose or destiny, there is no force in the universe that can stop you.

Spend five minutes at least three times a day reading your list and clearing your mind of stray thoughts. Focus on what you'd like to manifest and free yourself from fears or anxiety. When you have a clear picture in your mind, carry that image with you wherever you go. The clearer your vision, the stronger your intention. The stronger your intention, the more likely your desires will come to pass.

SAMPLE PRACTICE PLAN

Monday

Day Off

Tuesday

One Hour Practice

5 minutes of warm-up

20 minutes of full swing (technique focused)

20 minutes of pitching

15 minutes of putting

Wednesday

30 Minute Practice then Play 9 Hole Executive Course

5 minutes of warm-up

20 minutes of chipping

5 minutes of putting

Thursday

Two Hour Practice

5 minutes of warm-up

20 minutes of full swing (technique focused)

20 minutes of bunker play

20 minutes of pre-shot routine practice

20 minutes of shot making

20 minutes with the driver and - fairway woods

15 minutes of putting

Friday

30 Minute Practice and Play 9 Holes

5 minutes of warm-up

20 minutes with the irons

5 minutes of putting

Saturday

Play 18 holes

Sunday

Play 18 Holes

GOLF SKILLS EVALUATION

Pitching
(10 balls from 50 yards within 15 feet) _____ of 10

> 0 to 3   High Handicap Pitcher
> 4 to 6   Average Pitcher
> 7 to 10 Single Digit Handicap Pitcher

Short Irons (9 Iron to Lob Wedge)
(10 balls from 80 yards within 24 feet) _____ of 10

> 0 to 3   High Handicap Short Iron Player
> 4 to 6   Average Short Iron Player
> 7 to 10 Single Digit Handicap Short Iron Player

Mid Irons (5 Iron to 8 Iron)
(10 balls from 160 yards within 48 feet)_____ of 10

> 0 to 3   High Handicap Mid Iron Player
> 4 to 7   Average Mid Iron Player
> 8 to 10 Single Digit Handicap Mid Iron Player

Off the Tee with Driver
(10 balls from the tee into a 35 yard wide fairway)
_____ of 10

> 0 to 2   High Handicap Driver
> 3 to 5   Average Driver
> 6 to 10 Single Digit Handicap Driver

-Short Putts

(10 putts made from four feet) _____ of 10

> 0 to 5   High Handicap Short Putter
> 6 to 7   Average Short Putter
> 8 to 10 Single Digit Handicap Short Putter

- Long Putts

(10 putts from 35 within four feet) _____ of 10

> 0 to 6   High Handicap Long Putter
> 7 to 8   Average Long Putter
> 9 to 10 Single Digit Handicap Long Putter

- Chipping

(10 chips with 9 feet of carry and 35 feet total within four feet) _____ of 10

> 0 to 4   High Handicap Chipper
> 5 to 7   Average Chipper
> 8 to 10 Single Digit Handicap Chipper

- Bunker Play

(10 bunker shots from 35 feet within four feet) _____ of 10

> 0 to 3   High Handicap Bunker Player
> 4 to 6   Average Bunker Player
> 7 to 10 Single Digit Handicap Bunker Player

PRACTICE GRID

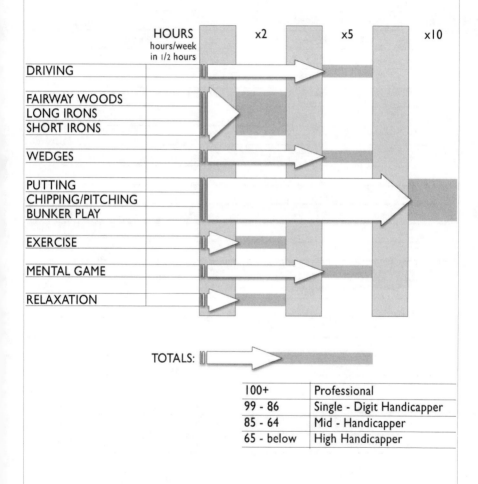

	HOURS hours/week in 1/2 hours	x2	x5	x10
DRIVING				
FAIRWAY WOODS				
LONG IRONS				
SHORT IRONS				
WEDGES				
PUTTING				
CHIPPING/PITCHING				
BUNKER PLAY				
EXERCISE				
MENTAL GAME				
RELAXATION				

TOTALS:

100+	Professional
99 - 86	Single - Digit Handicapper
85 - 64	Mid - Handicapper
65 - below	High Handicapper

NOTES

Breaking Golf's Unbreakable Barriers

QUOTES

"Golf is 100% mental and 100% physical."
                    -Ben Hogan

"Every putt is a straight putt."
                    -Bobby Locke

"Trust your muscles and hit the ball to the hole. Keep it simple."
                    -Harvey Penick

"If you worry about the ones you missed, you are going to keep missing them."
                    -Walter Hagan

"Sport does not build character. Sport reveals character."
                    -John Wooden

"Life is difficult. This is a great truth, one of the greatest truths. It is a great truth because once we truly see this truth, we transcend it. Once we truly know that life is difficult-once we truly understand and accept it-then life is no longer difficult. Because once it is accepted, the fact that life is difficult no longer matters."
                    -M. Scott Peck

"A man of character finds a special attractiveness in difficulty, since it is only by coming to grips with difficulty that he can realize his poten-tialities."
                    -Charles de Gaulle

"Adversity reveals genius, prosperity conceals it."
                    -Horace

"Sweet are the uses of adversity; Which, like the toad, ugly and venomous, Wears yet a precious jewel in his head..."
                    -William Shakespeare, As You Like It

"The ultimate measure of a man is not where he stands in moments of comfort and convenience, but where he stands at times of challenge and controversy."
                    -Martin Luther King, Jr.

"Great works are done when one is not calculating and thinking."
                    -Daisetz T. Suzuki

"If there is a purpose in life at all, there must be a purpose in suffering and dying. But no man can tell another what this purpose is. Each must find out for himself, and must accept the responsibility that his answer prescribes. If he succeeds, he will continue to grow in spite of his indignities."
                    -Gordon W. Allport

"A spiritually optimistic point of view holds that the universe is woven out of a fabric of love. Everything that is happening is ultimately for the good if we're willing to face it head-on and use our adversities for soul growth."
                    -Joan Borysenko

"Don't let the bad shots get to you. Don't let yourself become angry. The true scramblers are thick-skinned. And they always beat the whiners."
                    -Paul Runyan

"When I play my best golf, I feel as if I'm in a fog, standing back watching the earth in orbit with a golf club in my hands."
                    -Mickey Wright

"These greens are so fast I have to hold my putter over the ball and hit it with the shadow."

-Sam Snead

"Never break your putter and your driver in the same round or you're dead."

-Tommy Bolt

"Is my best friend in the bunker or is that bastard on the green?"

-Anon

"The swing is never learned. It is remembered."

- Steven Pressfield, The Legend of Baggar Vance

"The gem cannot be polished without friction, nor man perfected without trials."

-Confucius

"Hit it hard. It will land somewhere."

-Mark Calcavecchia

"No matter what happens-never give up a hole...In tossing in your cards after a bad beginning you also undermine your whole game, because to quit between tee and green is more habit-forming than drinking a highball before breakfast."

-Sam Snead

"A hungry dog hunts best."

-Lee Trevino

"You can talk to a fade but a hook won't listen."

-Lee Trevino

"Inspiration may be a form of superconsciousness, or perhaps of sub-consciousness- I wouldn't know. But I'm sure it is the antithesis of self-consciousness."

-Aaron Copland

"Desire, ask, believe, receive."

-Stella Terrill Mann

"If I had cleared the trees and drove the green, it would have been a great shot."

-Sam Snead

"To play any golf shot correctly requires an unwavering concentration. The most perfect swing in the world needs direction, and plenty of it, and when its possessor begins to do a little mental daisy picking, something always goes wrong."

-Bobby Jones

"Practice puts brains in your muscles."

-Sam Snead

"Nobody ever looked up and saw a good shot."

-Don Herold, Love That Golf

"By the time you get to your ball, if you don't know what to do with it, try another sport."

-Julius Boros

"Golf is very much like a love affair, if you take it seriously, it's no fun. If you do, it breaks your heart. Don't break your heart, but flirt with the possibility."

-Louise Suggs

"I play in the low 80's. If it's any hotter than that, I won't play."
                                            -Joe E. Louis

"When you don't play very often, you just don't know what is coming next."
                                            -Peter Thomson

"The trouble that most of us find with the modern matched set of clubs is that they don't really seem to know any more about the game than the old one's did!"
                                            -Robert Browning, A History of Golf

"Swing hard in case you hit it."
                                            -Dan Marino

"It took me seventeen years to get 3,000 hits in baseball. I did it in one afternoon on the golf course."
                                            -Hank Aaron

"Have you ever noticed what golf spells backwards?"
                                            -Al Boliska

"My favorite shots are the practice swing and the conceded putt. The rest can never be mastered."
                                            -Lord Robertson

"A rough should have high grass. When you go bowling they don't give you anything for landing in the gutter, do they?"
                                            -Lee Trevino

"Some say practice puts brains in your muscles; I say practice puts muscles in your brain."
                                            -Sam Snead

"Some people think of me as just plain lucky, and I can't argue with them. I would like to say, however, that a man might be walking around lucky and not know it unless he tries."
                          -Arnold Palmer

"Golf is the cruelest game, because eventually it will drag you out in front of the whole school, take your lunch money and slap you around."
                          -Rick Reilly
"When it's breezy, hit it easy."
                          -Davis Love, Jr.

"I look into their eyes, shake their hand, pat their back, and wish them luck, but I am thinking, 'I am going to bury you.'"
                          -Seve Ballesteros

"The quality of a person's life is in direct proportion to their commitment to excellence, regardless of their chosen field of endeavor."
                          -Vince Lombardi

"I screwed up. It's all on me. I know that. But losing this Masters is not the end of the world. I let this one get away, but I still have a pretty good life. I'll wake up tomorrow, still breathing, I hope. All these hiccups I have, they must be for a reason. All this is just a test. I just don't know what the test is yet."
                          -Greg Norman on the 1996 Masters

"You create your own luck by the way you play. There is no such luck as bad luck. Fate has nothing to do with success or failure, because that is a negative philosophy that indicts one's confidence, and I'll have no part in it."
                          -Greg Norman

"Psychic development cannot be accomplished by intention and will alone; it needs the attraction of the symbol."
                          -C.G. Jung

"The meeting of two eternities, the past and the future...is precisely the present moment."

-Henry David Thoreau

"Winners and losers are self-determined. Only the winners admit it."

-John Wooden

"Persistence requires heart."

-Eddie Merrins

"Great things are not done by impulse, but by a series of small things brought together."

-Vincent Van Gogh

"Think of yourself as on the threshold of unparalleled success. A whole clear, glorious life lies before you. Achieve! Achieve!"

- Andrew Carnegie

"He who has a why to live can bear with almost any how."

-Friedrich Nietzsche

"Hateful to me as are the gates of hell, is he who, hiding one thing in his heart, utters another."

-Homer

"Happiness is when what you think, what you say, and what you do are in harmony."

-Mahatma Gandhi

"You must be the change you wish to see in the world."

-Mohandas Karamchand Gandhi

"Everybody thinks of changing humanity and nobody thinks of changing himself."

-Leo Tolstoy

"It does not matter how slowly you go, as long as you do not stop."
-Confucius

"Creativity is 10% inspiration, 90% perspiration."
-Unknown

"When there is judgment, there is no room for love."
-Mother Teresa

"Don't let what you cannot do interfere with what you can do."
-John Wooden

"One meets his destiny often in the road he takes to avoid it."
-French Proverb

"We attract what we fear!"
-Anonymous

"Act as though it were impossible to fail."
-Dorothea Brand

"Try, there is no try. Only do or not do."
-Yoda

"The way to get started is to quit talking and begin doing."
-Walt Disney

"One hundred percent of the shots you don't take don't go in."
-Wayne Gretzky

"It does not matter how slowly you go, as long as you do not stop."
-Confucius

"Nothing is particularly hard if you divide it into small jobs."
-Henry Ford

"You can't build a reputation on what you're going to do."
-Henry Ford

"Achievement is largely the product of steadily raising one's levels of aspiration ... and expectation."
- Jack Nicklaus

"If you think you can, you can. And if you think you can't, you're right."
-Henry Ford

"He that is good with a hammer tends to think everything is a nail."
-Abraham Maslow

"Let no one come to you without leaving better and happier."
-Mother Teresa

"Life can be found only in the present moment. The past is gone, the future is not yet here, and if we do not go back to ourselves in the present moment, we cannot be in touch with life."
- Thich Nhat Hanh

"Life is a succession of lessons, which must be lived to be understood."
-Ralph Waldo Emerson

"The door to happiness opens outward."
-Anonymous

"Three things in human life are important: The first is to be kind. The second is to be kind. And the third is to be kind."
-Henry James

"To play well, you have to learn to channel the emotions, both the highs and the very lows."

-Pete Sampras

"Never change a winning game; always change a losing one."

-Bill Tilden

"The greatest efforts in sports...come when the mind is as still as a glass lake."

-Timothy Gallway

"I stay in the present, focusing on what I need to accomplish in the here and now."

-Tiger Woods

"All of us get knocked down, but it's the resiliency that really matters. All of us do well when things are going well, but the thing that distinguishes athletes is the ability to do well in great stress, urgency, and pressure."

-Roger Staubach

"I used to get out there and have a hundred swing thoughts. Now I try not to have any."

-Davis Love III

"One way to break up any kind of tension is good deep breathing."

-Byron Nelson

"If you can believe it, the mind can achieve it."

-Ronnie Lott

"It takes as much energy to wish as it does to plan."

-Eleanor Roosevelt

"Many people fail in life, not for lack of ability or brains or even courage but simply because they have never organized their energies around a goal."

-Elbert Hubbard

"Never mistake activity for achievement."

-John Wooden

"Make the most of yourself, for that is all there is of you."

-Ralph Waldo Emerson

"There's no substitute for guts."

-Paul "Bear" Bryant

"See the ball; hit the ball."

-Pete Rose

"It's lack of faith that makes people afraid of meeting challenges, and I believe in myself."

-Muhammad Ali

"Losing is no disgrace if you've given your best."

-Jim Palmer

"What lies behind us and what lies before us are tiny matters compared to what lies within us."

-Ralph Waldo Emerson

"Act like you expect to get into the end zone."

-Joe Paterno

"No army can withstand the strength of an idea whose time has come."

-Victor Hugo

"Act as though it were impossible to fail."

-Dorothea Brand

"Idleness is emptiness; the tree in which the sap is stagnant, remains fruitless."

-Hosea Ballou

"Show me a guy who's afraid to look bad, and I'll show you a guy you can beat every time."

-Lou Brock

"Confidence has to be the golfer's greatest single weapon...if he believes he can get the ball ino the hole, a lot of the time he will, even if his technique appears downright faulty."

-Jack Nicklaus

"Visualization enables us to conjure up confidence, boosting alignments or scenarios that assist us in freeing our minds from doubt, anxiety, or other inhibiting negative thoughts."

-Larry Miller, Golfing in the Zone

"Don't measure yourself by what you have accomplished, but by what you should have accomplished with your ability."

-John Wooden

"Whatever your ambitions in this game may be, unless you are prepared to invest a certain amount of time on the practice range, golf will continue to get the better of you."

-David Leadbetter

"I'm not saying you should whistle Summertime while you're hitting shots. But I do think that when you're carefree, you're relaxed, and when you're relaxed you swing freely."

-Fred Couples

"We will either find a way, or make one."
                    -Hannibal

"All that we are is the result of what we have thought."
                    -Buddha

"Setting a goal is not the main thing. It is deciding how you will go about achieving it and staying with that plan."
                    -Tom Landry

"Give me the wind, bad weather, bumpy greens, and slow play-it all gives me an advantage because I know I'm mentally prepared to handle it while a lot of other player's aren't."
                    -Dave Stockton

"I just see the shot and hit it."
                    -Tiger Woods

"Be Prepared."
                    -Boy Scout Motto

REFERENCES AND
ADDITIONAL
INFORMATION

To learn more about The Enneagram check out the following:

Helen Palmer. The Enneagram: Understanding Yourself and the Others in Your Life. Harper: San Francisco. 1988.

Don Richard Riso and Russ Hudson. Discovering Your Personality Type: The Essential Introduction to the Enneagram. Houghton Mifflin: Boston. 2003.

For mechanical assistance, contact a PGA Professional and consider the following:

John Andrisani. The Hogan Way: How to Apply Ben Hogan's Exceptional Swing and Shotmaking Genius to Your Own Game. Harper Collins: New York. 2000.

Other excellent books on the mental game:

Bob Cullen & Bob Rotella. Golf is a Game of Confidence. Simon & Schuster: New York. 1996.

Bob Rotella. Golf is Not a Game of Perfect. Simon & Schuster: New York. 1995.

Bob Rotella & Bob Cullen. The Golf of Your Dreams. Simon & Schuster: New York. 1997.

Dave Pelz. Dave Pelz's Short Game Bible: Master the Finesse Swing and Lower Your Score. Doubleday: New York. 1999.

A personality inventory designed to assist you with determining your personality Type is available at our Website - **www.innergame.org**, along with Bag Tags and gifts for your family and playing partners.

Additional copies of Inner Game: Breaking Golf's Unbreakable Barriers may also be purchased at www.innergame.org.

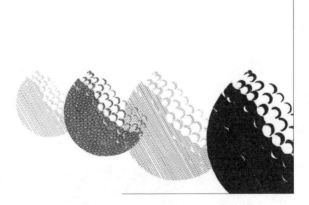

Dr. Mac Powell is a psychotherapist and golf professional with offices in Los Angeles and the Midwest. He can be reached for seminars and worldwide individual instruction at www.innergame.org.